measles ■ ■ ■ Report of the MMR Expert Group

Report of the MMR Expert Group

REPORT OF THE EXPERT GROUP ESTABLISHED BY THE SCOTTISH EXECUTIVE IN RESPONSE TO RECOMMENDATIONS SET OUT IN THE HEALTH AND COMMUNITY CARE COMMITTEE'S REPORT OF THE INQUIRY INTO ISSUES SURROUNDING THE ALLEGED RELATIONSHIP BETWEEN THE COMBINED MEASLES, MUMPS AND RUBELLA VACCINE AND AUTISM

Contents   Page

Chairman's Foreword

Mr Malcolm Chisholm MSP, Minister for Health and Community Care

Minister,

When Susan Deacon, the former Minister for Health, asked me to chair the MMR Expert Group, I was aware of the broad issues relating to MMR. The peaks and troughs of media interest; a growing public awareness of the tragedy of autism and Crohn's; the heartfelt campaigns of some parents of children with autism who are convinced that MMR is somehow responsible; news of outbreaks of measles both north and south of the Border – all rendered our task the more important.

Through chairing the work of the Expert Group I have learned a great deal. Much of that is set out in the pages that follow, in the hope that it may help others, as indeed it helped us. I recognise that Ministers and MSPs are not the only people interested in this work. Many organisations and parents expressed a strong interest over the last several months: I am very grateful to all who wrote or gave evidence.

The Group recognises that our Report only answers the questions we were asked. Research is ongoing, and more must be undertaken. Parents in Scotland may be confused as they hear claim and counter-claim in the media. This moving target was our context, as we addressed our remit. We trust that our Report will help all of us move forward and promote the rational debate proposed recently by the First Minister. We all share a common interest in the health and well being of all people in Scotland, especially our children.

Our Report contains a number of specific recommendations, which I hope you will consider and implement. Let me highlight three in particular:

- urgent action to improve the range and quality of services provided to, and for, children with autism and their families (as proposed by the Public Health Institute of Scotland);

- ongoing research into the causes of autism and Crohn's disease (as proposed by the Medical Research Council);

- better information for parents about MMR, and the diseases it protects us against.

The Expert Group tried to remain immune to the barrage of media speculation about its work and allegations of in-fighting. Such reports may sell newspapers; they were untrue. We have done what the Scottish Executive asked us to do – no more, no less – in accord with the remit given to us. I can assure you that all the issues within our remit were subjected to a thorough questioning and robust review, from a wide-ranging set of viewpoints. I believe that the benefits inherent in that approach are evident in the report that follows.

One aspect of our approach should be mentioned. We were keen to be aware of what parents with young children actually thought about MMR. We asked Scottish Health Feedback to help. Under its auspices a broadly representative Parents' Reference Group was created. These parents were involved at the start of our process and in providing helpful comment to our draft. We believe our Report is the more credible because of this involvement and we certainly took on board their views.

I must acknowledge the very positive contribution of each and every member of the Expert Group. Appointed by Scottish Ministers, the Expert Group deliberately embraced a range of disciplines and backgrounds. The membership included not only doctors and scientists, but also parents of children with autism or Crohn's and a health visitor; not only educationalists and those from the Scottish Society for Autism, the National Autistic Society, and the National Association for Colitis and Crohn's Disease, but also from the wider consumer movement. I am grateful for the support they provided, and for the knowledge, insight, diligence and compassion that they brought to our work.

The Expert Group would wish me to acknowledge the essential and impartial contributions to our task of your officials, Mr James Brown, Dr Elizabeth Stewart, Mr James Preston, and in particular Mr Joe Brown.

I have pleasure in submitting to you the unanimous report of the Expert Group you established.

The Very Revd Graham Forbes
Chairman, MMR Expert Group

Executive Summary

1. The Expert Group established by the Scottish Executive was asked:

"to consider the matters raised by the Health and Community Care Committee (HCCC) relating to immunisation against measles, mumps and rubella, with particular reference to:

a) describing the consequences of pursuing an alternative vaccination policy to MMR;

b) reviewing evidence on the apparent rise in the incidence of autism, taking account of the current work of the Medical Research Council;

c) describing the process of vaccine testing and the monitoring of adverse effects; and

d) in all its work, having regard to the role and remit of the Joint Committee on Vaccination and Immunisation, the Committee on Safety of Medicines and the Medicines Control Agency".

2. It is important to recognise that the remit of the Expert Group acknowledges both that other bodies advise Ministers on medicines, and immunisation policy, and that the Expert Group should consider those matters, to some degree, in the course of its work. The Expert Group gratefully acknowledges the support and assistance of all those individuals and organisations who contributed to that work, particularly the Parents' Reference Group. Full details are available on http://www.show.scot.nhs.uk/mmrexpertgroup/.

Autistic Spectrum Disorders

3. "Autism" is one of a spectrum of neurodevelopmental disorders which impair a person's capacity to communicate and interact with others. Thus, autistic spectrum disorder (ASD) is a complex, debilitating and lifelong set of conditions which manifests itself in many different ways.

4. *The Medical Research Council (MRC) Review of Autism Research* published on 13 December 2001 represents the most up-to-date expert assessment of the range and relative merit of current research evidence. The Expert Group endorses the conclusions reached by the MRC:

- ASD is considerably more common than has previously been recognised, with as many as 60 in 10,000 children affected;

- Methodological differences between studies, changes in diagnostic practice and public and professional awareness are likely causes of increases in prevalence. Whether these factors are sufficient to account for increased numbers of identified individuals, or whether there has been a rise in actual numbers affected, is as yet unclear.

- Current research evidence indicates that ASD has a variety of possible genetic and environmental risk factors which, acting together, may cause the disorder. As such, key issues for future research include case-definition, the roles and interplay between genetic and environmental risk factors, causal pathways and mechanisms, and new approaches to treatment.

5.   The Expert Group acknowledges, like the HCCC, the MRC and others, that the current scientific evidence does not support the hypothesised link between the MMR vaccine and autism.

6.   The Expert Group also considered the range and quality of services required for, and provided to, such families, and how these might be improved, supported by the *Public Health Institute of Scotland (PHIS) Needs Assessment Report on Autistic Spectrum Disorders*. The Expert Group strongly endorses that report's findings and conclusions and looks to the Scottish Executive for action.

7.   ASD is diagnosed on the basis of qualitative abnormalities in social, communicative and imaginative behaviours, and the presence of repetitive and stereotyped patterns of interests and activities. Diagnosis is therefore an involved and complicated matter. Evidence presented to the Expert Group supports the conclusion that diagnosis remains, for many, time-consuming and traumatic, and that, generally, health, social care and education professionals who do not specialise in ASD need up-to-date information and knowledge, and consistent national and local structures, in order to deliver improved, effective and integrated services that meet the varied needs of individuals with autism and their families.

Crohn's Disease

8.   Crohn's disease is a form of inflammatory bowel disease (sometimes referred to as IBD). The most recent estimate of the prevalence of Crohn's disease in children aged less than 16 years is 1.37 cases per 10,000 population in Scotland.

9.   We do not know what causes Crohn's disease. Epidemiological data have emphasised the importance of both environmental and genetic factors. Which precise environmental factors trigger the onset of Crohn's disease are not known. The measles virus is one of the possible environmental triggers suggested as causing Crohn's disease, and some researchers have suggested a possible connection between MMR vaccine, bowel disease and autism. All relevant research has been reviewed by a number of expert groups, and, while there may be abnormalities of the bowel in some children with ASD, the current scientific evidence does not support the suggestion that they are either a feature of, or involved in, the pathogenesis of ASD.

Vaccine Testing and Monitoring

10.   The Committee on Safety of Medicines (CSM) is an independent advisory committee which advises Health Ministers on the quality, efficacy and safety of medicines in order to ensure that appropriate public health standards are met and maintained.

11.   The UK Medicines Control Agency (MCA) is an Executive Agency of the Department of Health (in England). Its primary objective is to safeguard public health by ensuring that all medicines on the UK market meet appropriate standards of safety, quality and efficacy.

12. Medicines, which meet standards of safety, quality and efficacy, are granted a marketing authorisation, which is necessary before they can be prescribed or sold. The MCA carries out pre-marketing assessment of the medicine's safety, quality and efficacy, examining all the research and test results in detail, before a decision is made on whether the product should be granted a marketing authorisation.

13. Before a product is marketed, experience of its safety and efficacy is limited to its use in clinical trials. The conditions under which patients are studied, pre-marketing, do not necessarily reflect the way the medicine will be used in hospital or in general practice once it is marketed. Consequently, there is a continued need for vigilance to detect adverse effects that become apparent when the medicine is more widely used.

14. The MCA is responsible for the UK's spontaneous adverse drug reaction reporting scheme (called the "Yellow Card" reporting scheme) to which doctors report suspected adverse drug reactions. The scheme provides an important early warning of suspected adverse reactions to medicines. The work of the MCA in pharmacovigilance is conducted in a world-wide context, with close links and increasing information transfer with other regulatory authorities, for example the Food and Drug Administration (FDA) in the USA.

15. The submissions presented to the Expert Group fully support the conclusion that MMR was appropriately and rigorously tested before introduction, consistent with standards and science relevant at the time. The Expert Group also recognises that the MCA continually monitors the safety of MMR vaccines in clinical practice and, if necessary, updates the marketing authorisation and product information if and when new data become available.

16. The Medicines Act 1968 contains an exemption which allows the supply of unlicensed relevant medicinal products for human use (commonly known as "specials") in response to a genuine unsolicited order, formulated in accordance with the specification of a doctor or dentist, and for use by his individual patients on the doctor's or dentist's direct personal responsibility. Responsibility for deciding whether an individual patient has "special needs" which the licensed product cannot meet is a matter for the doctor responsible for the patient's care. There are single component measles, mumps and rubella vaccines licensed in the UK, but the licensed single measles and mumps vaccines are not currently marketed by their licence holders in the UK. The MCA has confirmed that the importation of unlicensed monocomponent vaccines is not uncommon.

The Consequences of Alternative Vaccination Policies

18. The Expert Group was asked by the Executive to describe the consequences of pursuing an alternative vaccination policy to MMR and, as such, recognised that it was not expected or required to review MMR policy or the current immunisation programme.

19. The success of immunisation against measles, mumps and rubella has led to a decline in the incidence of these diseases. As such, the associated risks may not be fully appreciated:

Complications of measles	Complications of mumps	Complications of rubella
• ear infection (1 in 20) • pneumonia/bronchitis (1 in 25) • convulsions (1 in 200) • diarrhoea (1 in 6) • meningitis/encephalitis (1 in 1000) • conditions affecting blood clotting (1 in 6000) • late onset subacute sclerosing panencephalitis (SSPE) (1 in 8000 children under 2 years) • deaths (1–2 deaths in 1000 reported cases in recent years)	• viral meningitis (1 in 20) • encephalitis (1 in 1000) • permanent hearing loss (1 in 20,000) • inflammation of testicles (4 in 10 adult males) • inflammation of ovaries	• encephalitis (1 in 6000) • birth defects (90% chance baby will have birth defects if mother catches rubella early in pregnancy). Birth defects include blindness, deafness, learning difficulties and heart disease • conditions affecting blood clotting (1 in 3000)

20. Serious complications have been reported for one in 15 notified cases of measles, but are more common and severe in chronically ill children. In recent years, one to two people in every 1000 with reported measles infection have died from it. Death from measles is highest in children under 1 year – a group of children who do not receive MMR vaccine – and in those who are immunosuppressed, due to disease (e.g. leukaemia) or treatment (e.g. organ transplantation) and cannot receive MMR vaccine (or indeed single vaccines). Mumps can have serious complications, with neurological involvement in 10–20% of cases. Pre-immunisation, it was one of the main causes of acquired sensorineural deafness in childhood. Rubella is generally a mild illness, which, if acquired by mothers in early pregnancy, nevertheless can have devastating effects on unborn children.

21. Very rarely, in common with any medical intervention, MMR can cause serious adverse effects. Such adverse effects are significantly more common following the natural disease.

Conditions	Rate after natural disease	Rate after first dose of MMR
Febrile convulsions (temperature fits)	1 in 200	1 in 1000
Meningitis/encephalitis	1 in 1000 (measles, mumps encephalitis) 1 in 20 (mumps meningitis) 1 in 6000 (rubella encephalitis)	less than 1 in 1,000,000
Conditions affecting blood clotting (ITP)	1 in 3000 (rubella) 1 in 6000 (measles)	1 in 22,000
Severe allergic response (anaphylaxis)	–	1 in 100,000
SSPE (a delayed complication of measles that causes brain damage and death)	1 in 8000 (children under 2)	0
Deaths	1 in 2500 to 1 in 5000 (measles; higher in children under 1) 1–2 in 1000 for measles in recent years	0

22. There are of course some children who should not have MMR, at all, or at a particular time. For example, children with untreated cancer or diseases of the immune system, those receiving immunosuppressive therapy or high dose steroids cannot be given MMR (or the corresponding single vaccines). In such circumstances, children depend upon the population immunity that is a product of high immunisation uptake. In contrast, if a child is suffering from an acute illness, immunisation would be postponed until recovery has occurred.

23. The Expert Group accepted and endorsed without reservation the high-level strategic objectives of immunisation: prevention of diseases at the individual level; control of disease at the population level; and elimination or eradication of disease. The Expert Group developed a framework of principles to guide its thinking, and consider that future debate could be informed and facilitated by a Joint Committee on Vaccination and Immunisation (JCVI) framework of principles for immunisation policy.

24. The Expert Group considered five immunisation policies, which might be considered as an alternative to the current policy:

- no immunisation;
- compulsory immunisation;
- deferral of MMR;
- a choice between either MMR or single vaccines;
- single vaccines.

Before addressing these options it is important to recognise a very practical consideration, which is that, although single antigen measles and mumps vaccine were previously available in the UK, they are not currently manufactured to UK licence specifications.

25. None of the submissions presented to the Expert Group question the merit of immunisation against measles, mumps and rubella, more generally. There is therefore a clear and overwhelming consensus that a "no immunisation" policy is not tenable. Similarly, none of the submissions presented to the Expert Group supported compulsion or the option of single vaccines replacing MMR in the childhood vaccination programme.

26. The Expert Group recognises that deferring MMR immunisation is in effect an option. However, the Expert Group concluded such a policy is not consistent with key elements of its framework of principles for immunisation policy. It is not supported by current scientific evidence, and it leaves children unprotected and at greater risk of infection for longer than is necessary.

27. The Expert Group recognises that some parents express a wish to be given the capacity to select either MMR or single vaccines for their children. The case for making single vaccines available by popular choice, as opposed to the clinical judgement of a health professional (as at present), cannot however be sustained on the basis of the available scientific evidence. There is no proven scientific link between the MMR vaccine and autism or Crohn's disease. Another important factor is that even if there were substantive scientific evidence to support the original hypothesised link between autism and measles virus, there is no evidence that the single vaccine option would actually be any safer. Similarly, the scientific evidence supports the conclusion that the MMR component viruses do not interfere with each other. The efficacy of MMR and single vaccines is the same, subject to issues of manufacture and quality control, but the comparative effectiveness of single vaccines is more open to question. It is clear that, if single vaccines were made available in this way, protection at individual and population level would depend on:

i)   the extent to which this would result in increased vaccine uptake by those who refuse to accept the safety of MMR and leave their children, and others, unprotected;

ii) the extent to which this would change the vaccine uptake decisions taken by those who currently accept MMR;

iii) the extent to which multiple visits would result in increased default; and

iv) the extent to which leaving a space between vaccines rather than using concurrent administration would open up a window within which temporarily unvaccinated children would be at significantly elevated vulnerability to infection.

Recommendations

28. In the course of addressing its remit the Expert Group identified a range of possible and desirable changes to existing arrangements. The Group therefore recommends that:

a) The Scottish Executive and the Medical Research Council should work together to drive forward and fund, as appropriate, the full research agenda outlined in the final chapter of the MRC Review of Autism Research, which was informed by the concerns of parents and consumers. Parents and other representatives of those with autism must continue to play a key role in developing research strategies (paragraph 2.40).

b) The Scottish Executive and the Medical Research Council should, in pursuing that research agenda, seek to maximise international collaboration (paragraph 2.41).

c) The Scottish Executive should consult widely, in order to publish a firm timetable for addressing all of the detailed recommendations set out in the PHIS *Autistic Spectrum Disorders Needs Assessment Report* (paragraphs 2.48 and 2.49), and in particular those relating to the:

- development and implementation of improved evidence-based approaches to the diagnosis and management of ASD;

- integrated joint planning, delivery and review of related health, education and social care services, for children, parents and adults, in which context people with autism, or parents and other representatives of those with autism, should have a role;

- need for a more coherent and systematic approach to training health, education and social care professionals, better and in appropriate numbers;

- development of a database of people with ASD in Scotland.

d) The Scottish Executive and the Medical Research Council should work together to drive forward and fund, as appropriate, further research into inflammatory bowel disorders in children (paragraph 3.16).

e) The Medicines Control Agency should continue to work closely with the European Union, and appropriate corresponding bodies in individual member states, to improve collaboration and monitoring of vaccine safety issues, and regularly review the operation, management and voluntary nature of the "Yellow Card" system in the light of such developments (paragraph 4.18).

f) The Scottish Executive should ensure that (paragraph 4.35):

- vaccination records relating to individual patients should include details of the name and batch number of the vaccine administered;

- a national lifelong vaccination record is developed, to allow identification of the immunisation status of an individual throughout the health service – irrespective of age group and independent of setting;

- NHS Health Boards put in place adequate quality assurance mechanisms to ensure accuracy and completeness of recording of vaccination data.

g) The Committee on Safety of Medicines and the Joint Committee on Vaccination and Immunisation should, taking account of ongoing and future research into the causes of IBD and autism, continue to keep vaccination contraindications under review (paragraph 5.25).

h) The Joint Committee on Vaccination and Immunisation should (paragraph 5.29):

- develop and publish core principles for immunisation policy in order to provide all interested parties with a clear framework against which future policy options might be assessed in an open and transparent manner; and

- continue to publish the conclusion of its regular reviews of the scientific evidence relating to the safety and efficacy of MMR, and seek to improve upon existing arrangements for publicising that material.

i) Health Ministers (in the UK Government and devolved administrations) should urgently implement existing plans to extend arrangements for appointing members to the Joint Committee on Vaccination and Immunisation who are non-medical experts and/or members of the general public (paragraph 5.31).

j) The Scottish Executive should take steps to improve the level and quality of information available to parents whose children are due to be immunised against measles, mumps and rubella (paragraphs 5.21 and 5.32), by:

- ensuring that all parents receive basic factual information about MMR (for example, contraindications, the risks posed by measles, mumps and rubella, and the risks of adverse reactions) with the invitation to bring their child for vaccination;

- ensuring that all parents know that they can, and should, discuss any related questions with their GP or health visitor in order to make an informed choice about vaccination;

- asking HEBS to evaluate and develop *the MMR discussion pack*, in order to maintain and enhance the currency and accuracy of the information, training and support provided to GPs and other health professionals, in relation to the medical science underpinning the immunisation programme;

- requiring NHS Boards to put in place systematic arrangements for providing further advice to parents who, despite discussions with their GP or other health professional, have concerns and questions about MMR or the particular circumstances of their child.

k) The Scottish Executive should ensure that appropriate resources are provided to allow the Scottish Centre for Infection and Environmental Health to carry forward research, in collaboration with the University of Strathclyde, with the aim of developing mathematical models, which might help demonstrate the range of possible outcomes, for the population as a whole, arising out of immunisation decisions made by individual parents (paragraph 5.47).

1 Introduction

Each chapter begins with a box containing a short description of its content, and ends with a summary of key points.

This chapter describes:

- why the Expert Group was established and what it was asked to do (paragraphs 1.1 to 1.10);

- how the members of the Expert Group were appointed (paragraphs 1.11 to 1.16 and Annex A); and

- how the work of the Expert Group was taken forward in an open and inclusive way, and the individuals and organisations that contributed (paragraphs 1.17 to 1.33).

Background and Remit

1.1 Combined measles, mumps and rubella (MMR) vaccines were introduced into the UK routine childhood immunisation programme[I] in 1988. Initially, only one MMR dose was given, but a two-dose immunisation schedule with measles, mumps and rubella vaccine has existed in the UK since October 1996 (the first dose is given at 12–15 months and the second dose at 3–5 years).

1.2 Since 1998, however, there have been speculation and controversy surrounding the MMR vaccination focusing on a possible connection to inflammatory bowel disease and autism. This emerged as a result of the work of the Inflammatory Bowel Disease Study Group at the Royal Free Hospital and School of Medicine. In the early 1990s, they first suggested that the measles virus may be present in the bowel of individuals with inflammatory bowel disease. This work proved controversial as the findings could not be replicated in the peer-reviewed literature by others in the field. In 1998, the group published a paper describing 12 children with autism and an apparent novel form of bowel disease, and in eight of the children the onset of behavioural problems was linked to the time when MMR was administered. A press conference, held at the time of publication of this paper, created adverse publicity for the MMR vaccine.

1.3 Subsequent epidemiological studies of large numbers of children with autism have not found evidence of a link with MMR[1]. Similarly, reviews of both autism and MMR have not supported the assertion that MMR is in some way a trigger for autism or inflammatory bowel disease[2].

[I] For the purposes of this report the terms "immunisation" and "vaccination" should be considered largely interchangeable, consistent with common usage. The Expert Group acknowledges that the terms have more precise, and different, meanings in a professional, scientific or medical context.

1.4 Despite these studies, the public and media reaction has been somewhat different. Some 3000 parents who believe that their children have been damaged by the MMR vaccine are pursuing a legal action against the manufacturers. And, over time, a minority of parents in Scotland, and elsewhere in the UK, has decided to reject or postpone MMR immunisation, leaving their children, and others, at greater risk of contracting measles, mumps or rubella. This is illustrated below.

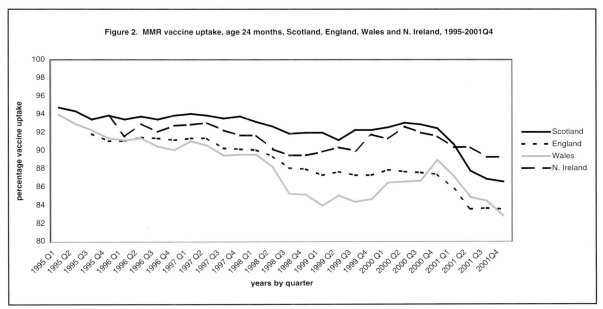

Figure 2. MMR vaccine uptake, age 24 months, Scotland, England, Wales and N. Ireland, 1995-2001Q4

(provided by SCIEH, using figures provided by ISD (Scotland) and PHLS CDSC (England, Wales and Northern Ireland)

1.5 In March 2000, the Public Petitions Committee considered Petition PE 145 by Mr Bill Welsh, which called for the Scottish Parliament to take a range of actions with regard to medical conditions arising from immunisations, against the background of that controversy and continuing concern about the public health implications. The petition was passed to the Health and Community Care Committee for further consideration.

1.6 The Health and Community Care Committee's 8th Report[3] stated that:

"on the basis of currently available evidence, there is no proven scientific link between the measles, mumps and rubella vaccine and autism or Crohn's disease and therefore the Committee has no reason to doubt the safety of the MMR vaccine. The Committee does not recommend any change in the current immunisation programme at this time".

The Committee also suggested that an Expert Group should be established to consider a range of questions relating to the concerns voiced by parents.

1.7 In its formal response[4] the Scottish Executive agreed to establish an Expert Group *"to consider the matters raised by the Health and Community Care Committee relating to immunisation against measles, mumps and rubella, with particular reference to:*

a) *describing the consequences of pursuing an alternative vaccination policy to MMR;*

b) *reviewing evidence on the apparent rise in the incidence of autism, taking account of the current work of the Medical Research Council;*

c) *describing the process of vaccine testing and the monitoring of adverse effects; and*

d) *in all its work, having regard to the role and remit of the Joint Committee on Vaccination and Immunisation, the Committee on Safety of Medicines and the Medicines Control Agency".*

1.8 The "matters raised by the Health and Community Care Committee" are largely defined by a series of questions posed by the Committee, which broadly underpin the formal remit of the Expert Group. The questions, and appropriate answers, are set out in Chapter 6.

1.9 It is, however, important to recognise that the remit of the Expert Group acknowledges both that other existing bodies advise Ministers on medicines, and immunisation policy, and that the Group would consider those matters, to some degree, in the course of its work.

1.10 Equally, it is worth acknowledging the shifting context for the Expert Group's work following the news of measles outbreaks in parts of England and in Scotland, early in 2002. The Public Health Laboratory Service has confirmed 95 cases of measles, with the majority (73) occurring in London. In Scotland, the Scottish Centre for Infection and Environmental Health (SCIEH) confirmed three cases of measles in Fife in March 2002 – the first such cases for 2 years.

Membership

1.11 The HCCC report stated that *"membership of the group will be decided by the Scottish Executive but should include representatives from the Scottish Society for Autism"*.

1.12 The Executive's response of 29 June confirmed that the Chairman of the Expert Group would be The Very Revd Graham Forbes, Provost of St Mary's Cathedral, Edinburgh.

1.13 The Executive then consulted the Chairman, and a range of professional and voluntary bodies, including in particular the Scottish Society for Autism, about the selection of additional members. The Executive also had regard to *Guidelines 2000: Scientific Advice And Policy Making*[5], which states that:

"Departments should draw on a sufficiently wide range of the best expert sources, both within and outside Government. These might include not only eminent individuals, learned societies, advisory committees, or consultants, but also professional bodies, public sector research establishments, lay members of advisory groups, consumer groups and other stakeholder bodies. As all experts will come to issues with views shaped to some extent by their own interests and experience, departments should also consider how to avoid unconscious bias, by ensuring that there is a good balance in terms of the type of institutions and organisations from which the experts are sought. Experts from other disciplines, not necessarily scientific, should also be invited to contribute, to ensure that the evidence is subjected to a sufficiently questioning review from a wide-ranging set of viewpoints.

Departments should ask prospective experts to follow the seven principles of public life as set out by the Committee on Standards in Public Life, which include the obligation to declare any private interests relating to their public duties. Departments should judge whether these interests could undermine the credibility or independence of the advice.

Where departments conclude that the potential conflicts of interest are not likely to undermine the credibility or independence of the advice, the relevant declarations of interests should, as a minimum, be made available to anyone who is proposing to act in reliance upon the advice. Departments will also need to consider whether it is appropriate to make the declarations more widely available."

1.14 Consistent with that, and the HCCC report, Mrs Jane Hook, Dr Clare Brogan and Mrs Gillian Hamer-Hodges were appointed to represent the interests, expertise and membership of the Scottish Society for Autism, the National Autistic Society, and the National Association for Colitis and Crohn's Disease, respectively. Details of the full membership of the Group were announced on 28 August 2001, the date of the first meeting.

1.15 The members of the Expert Group subsequently expressed a wish to broaden the membership in order to extend further their knowledge and understanding of matters relating to the diagnosis of autistic spectrum disorders, and the related provision of care. As a result, the Executive invited Dr Kenneth Aitken and Dr Gordon Bell to join the Expert Group, in a personal capacity, and they participated fully from November 2001.

1.16 The complete list of members and a separate summary of declared interests are at Annex 1.

Timetable and Process

1.17 The Expert Group met for the first time on 28 August 2001, and on eight subsequent occasions to consider relevant evidence and prepare this report.

1.18 A number of individuals and organisations provided oral and written submissions at those meetings:

> The Medicines Control Agency
>
> Ms J Muirie, The Public Health Institute of Scotland
>
> The Medical Research Council
>
> Mr A J Wakefield (formerly Royal Free and University College Medical School)
>
> Action Against Autism (Mr W Welsh, accompanied and assisted by Mr D Thrower, Dr P Copp and Dr K Aitken)
>
> Dr S Davies, Borders NHS Health Board
>
> Scottish Centre for Infection and Environmental Health and the University of Strathclyde (Dr C Bramley and Mr Peterson)
>
> Ms J E Baines, Highland Region Education Department
>
> Professor C Gillberg, University of Gothenburg
>
> Dr D A C Elliman, St George's Hospital, London
>
> Professor J Satsangi, University of Edinburgh.

Consultation

1.19 In week commencing 17 September 2001, adverts were placed in the *Health Service Journal, Aberdeen Press & Journal, The Scotsman, The Herald* and *Daily Record*. The adverts gave the full remit of the Expert Group and invited relevant contributions from individuals and organisations.

1.20 In response to that consultation process written submissions were provided by:

> Faculty of Public Health Medicine
>
> Royal College of General Practitioners
>
> Royal College of Nursing – Scottish Board
>
> Royal College of Physicians
>
> Royal College of Physicians of Edinburgh

Royal College of Paediatrics and Child Health – Scottish Committee

Royal College of Physicians and Surgeons Glasgow

Royal College of General Practitioners (Scotland)

Renfrewshire Autism and Asperger Group

Sense Scotland

Dr N Waugh

Mr R Miles

Mr D Thrower

Mrs S Campbell

Ms D Taylor

Dr A Clegg

Mr V Arcari

Ms A Laverty

Ms Y Gowans

Mr B Barreto.

1.21 The Expert Group gratefully acknowledges the support and assistance of all those individuals and organisations who contributed. Full details of their submissions[II] are available on http://www.show.scot.nhs.uk/mmrexpertgroup/.

Parents' Reference Group

1.22 As part of that process of consultation, the Expert Group established a broadly representative Parents' Reference Group to both inform its deliberations (by identifying priority issues relevant to its remit) and provide constructive comment on emerging conclusions.

1.23 Scottish Health Feedback (SHF), an independent research organisation which has been involved in several studies looking at parents' and health professionals' opinions about immunisation in general, and MMR in particular, managed this element of the work. SHF identified parents who might wish to be included in the Reference Group and worked with them to assess their priorities in relation to MMR and their views on the value of an earlier draft of this report. Full details of the contribution made by the Parents' Reference Group are set out in the reports prepared by Scottish Health Feedback. The reports are available on http://www.show.scot.nhs.uk/mmrexpertgroup/.

1.24 The Expert Group gratefully acknowledges the very valuable contribution of the Parents' Reference Group.

[II] Except where permission to publish in full was withheld for good reason, for example, pending publication in a peer-reviewed journal.

1.25 Taking account of the views of the Parents' Reference Group in particular, and others including the Health and Community Care Committee, this report seeks to either provide, or highlight the availability of, good, clear and concise information about autism, about MMR and about single vaccines. In this context, the Expert Group acknowledges that the *MMR discussion pack*[6], produced in 2001 by the Scottish Executive, the Scottish Centre for Infection and Environmental Health, and the Health Education Board for Scotland, sets out some facts about MMR in a way that helps health professionals and parents to explore any concerns together.

Evaluation of evidence

1.26 The Expert Group acknowledges that the process of evaluating evidence for the causation of disease is not easy. Although not formally tasked with doing this, the Expert Group was very aware that the background to its remit included concerns about the relationship between MMR, autism and bowel disease.

1.27 The Expert Group received submissions that addressed the issue of associations between these three. However, association is not causation, and it acknowledged the likely contribution of both genetic and environmental factors to the causation of autism and bowel disease, and the interaction within and between them. The question of definitions and the possibility of multiple causes were also acknowledged and are discussed below.

1.28 To determine the cause(s) of a disease or syndrome, certain scientific criteria must be satisfied, and the processes of evaluation of evidence observed. To evaluate biomedical (scientific) evidence both inductive and deductive methods are customarily used. The inductive method involves the amassing of evidence to support a prior hypothesis, while the deductive method tests a hypothesis by trying to falsify it. Generally the latter is regarded as a more powerful and secure route to scientific certainty, but both require systematic unbiased collection of information, through observation and experiment, in different populations and using a variety of appropriate study designs, in order to elucidate the relationship between proposed causes and the conditions in question.

1.29 In the evaluation of evidence there is a hierarchy of study designs or "statements of evidence" available to the investigator, ranging from the meta-analysis of randomised controlled trials, through experimental studies to case series. Evidence obtained from "expert" committee reports or opinions and/or clinical experience of "respected authorities" is regarded as the weakest source of evidence in this hierarchy[7].

1.30 The Expert Group was greatly assisted by the *MRC Review of Autism Research* (2001)[8], which was published during the course of its deliberations. The section (paragraphs 84 to 88) on "Criteria to Assess Causality" deals in some detail with the processes and difficulties in identifying possible causative relations between MMR, autism and bowel disease.

1.31 The Expert Group received verbal and written submissions which sought to both support and refute causative relations between MMR, autism and bowel disease. Much of this has been reviewed by the MRC, and some is discussed in Chapter 2 of this report.

Other matters

1.32 In the course of addressing its remit and considering the submissions presented by others, the Expert Group has, on occasion, reflected on the fact that it is not a scientific expert group in a conventional sense, because its members have a broader range of experience and expertise. This recognises the many different facets of the remit. The Expert Group considers that this inclusive and multidisciplinary approach has enabled an holistic, searching and coherent examination of the issues.

1.33 The HCCC report stated that *"it is important to view this Report as the beginning of a process of investigation and clarification of all the issues and strategies surrounding the combined vaccine, rather than as a definitive set of conclusions"*. The Expert Group agrees that its own report should also be viewed as a stage in an ongoing process, particularly in relation to the causes and treatment of ASD.

Chapter 1 – Summary of Key Points

This report sets out the views of the Expert Group established "to consider the matters raised by the Health and Community Care Committee (HCCC) relating to immunisation against measles, mumps and rubella, with particular reference to:

- *describing the consequences of pursuing an alternative vaccination policy to MMR;*

- *reviewing evidence on the apparent rise in the incidence of autism, taking account of the current work of the Medical Research Council (MRC);*

- *describing the process of vaccine testing and the monitoring of adverse effects; and*

- *in all its work, having regard to the role and remit of the Joint Committee on Vaccination and Immunisation, the Committee on Safety of Medicines and the Medicines Control Agency".*

The remit makes clear that other bodies advise Ministers on medicines, and immunisation policy.

The Expert Group was determined to complete that task in an open and inclusive way, and to undertake a thorough, questioning review from a wide-ranging set of viewpoints. It gratefully acknowledges the support and assistance of all those individuals and organisations who contributed to this work, particularly the Parents' Reference Group.

Details of the members and their declared interests (also at Annex 1), the consultation process adopted, and the submissions from individuals and organisations are available on http://www.show.scot.nhs.uk/mmrexpertgroup/.

The Expert Group believes that this report should be viewed as a stage in an ongoing process, particularly in relation to the causes and treatment of ASD.

2 Autistic Spectrum Disorders

This chapter describes:

- autistic spectrum disorders (ASD) (paragraphs 2.5 to 2.7);

- how common ASDs are, based on current evidence (paragraphs 2.8 to 2.14);

- what we know, at present, about the causes of ASD (paragraphs 2.15 to 2.42);

- how ASDs are diagnosed (paragraphs 2.43 to 2.46); and

- the importance of improving the educational, social and health services provided to individuals with ASD (paragraphs 2.47 to 2.51).

Introduction

2.1   The Expert Group was asked to review evidence on the apparent rise in the incidence of autism, taking account of the current work of the Medical Research Council (MRC).

2.2   The *MRC Review of Autism Research*[8], published on 13 December 2001, provides a substantive and rigorous academic framework for the related work of the Expert Group. The Expert Group acknowledges that the MRC Review represents the most up-to-date expert assessment of the range and relative merit of current research evidence. The Expert Group also welcomes the way in which the MRC sought to take account, throughout the review, and in its findings, of relevant "grey" evidence (from parents, case records, and other "non-scientific" sources) in order to gain a more holistic perspective on what is known at present.

2.3   However, the Expert Group was also keen to take account of parents' expressed need for clear and concise information about autism: what it is; how it develops; how it can be recognised; and what are its causes.

2.4   The Group was also motivated by submissions presented by parents of children with autism, and others, to consider the range and quality of services required for, and provided to, such families, and how these might be improved. This falls more properly within the ambit of the Public Health Institute of Scotland (PHIS) *Needs Assessment Report on Autistic Spectrum Disorders*[9], but the Group wished to endorse strongly that report's findings and conclusions.

Autism and Autistic Spectrum Disorders

2.5   Autism is one of a set of neurodevelopmental disorders which impair a person's capacity to communicate and interact with others. It is a term which has been in use for over 60 years, but is now, increasingly, being replaced by the concept of an autistic spectrum, covering a range of ability levels and manifestations of a set of common criteria: qualitative impairments in social, communicative and imaginative development. Autistic spectrum disorder is a complex, debilitating and lifelong set of conditions which manifests itself in many different ways.

2.6 Consistent with that, international classification systems (the World Health Organization's "International Classification of Diseases", 10th edition (ICD-10)[10] and the American Psychiatric Association's "Diagnostic and Statistical Manual", 4th edition (DSM-IV)[11]) recognise several sub-groups of ASD and other pervasive development disorders. For example:

ICD 10 (World Health Organization, Geneva, 1994)

F84.0 Childhood autism

F84.1 Atypical autism

    F84.10 Atypicality in age at onset

    F84.11 Atypicality in symptomatology

    F84.12 Atypicality in age at onset and symptomatology

F84.2 Rett syndrome

F84.3 Other childhood disintegrative disorder

F84.4 Overactive disorder associated with mental retardation and stereotyped movements

F84.5 Asperger's syndrome

F84.8 Other pervasive developmental disorders

F84.9 Pervasive developmental disorders unspecified

2.7 The Expert Group recognises that any formal definition will fail to capture the impact of ASD on any particular individual and family. This is covered in the following sections dealing with diagnosis and services.

Prevalence and Incidence

According to recent reviews, there appears fairly good agreement that the autism spectrum disorders affect approximately 60, and narrowly-defined autism 10–30, per 10,000 children under 8.

MRC Review of Autism Research

2.8 Prevalence measures the number of individuals with a condition at a point in time or over a defined period. It is related to incidence and duration of disease, and may increase as a result of increasing numbers or longer survival with a diagnosis. Incidence measures the development of "new" cases and is usually studied for disorders with clear onset.

2.9 The Expert Group was asked to review evidence on the apparent rise in the incidence of ASD, but has focused instead on the prevalence because that has been the focus, for the most part, of epidemiological studies of ASD.

2.10 Reviewing evidence on the apparent rise in the prevalence of autism was relatively straightforward. Submissions presented to the Expert Group signalled a strong consensus, consistent with the findings of the MRC Review. The following table shows how epidemiological evidence has progressed.

Autistic Spectrum Disorders – Review of Literature

Year	Authors	Type	Measurements	Findings	Other Information
1979	Wing & Gould[12]	Study	Prevalence (children)	5 per 10,000 children ("classic autism") 15 per 10,000 children broader ASD)	
1993	Wing[13]	Review of 16 studies	Prevalence (children)	3.3 to 16 per 10,000 children ("typical autism" defined variously)	
1993	Ehlers & Gillberg[14]	Two-stage total population study	Prevalence (children aged 7–16)	Min. 36 per 10,000 children with AS plus equivalent number who did not meet full criteria for ASD	
1999	Fombonne[15]	Review of 23 epidemiological studies (1966–98)	Prevalence (children)	Minimum of 18.7 per 10,000 children (all ASD except AS)	
1999	Gillberg & Wing[16]	Review of epidemiological studies of prevalence of autism (1966–1998)	Prevalence (children up to 18)	0.7 to 31 per 10,000 Estimate made of 1 per 1000 children for classic autism	Use of Kanner's strict criteria seems to give significantly lower rates than DSM or ICD criteria.
2000	Powell & Edwards[17]	Study of incidence rates		4.8/10,000 p.a. for pre-5 children for "other ASD" (1996) 3.5/10,000 p.a. for pre-5 children for "classic" autism	Small study so may not be generalisable
2000	Baird et al.[18]	Follow-up population study of prevalence	Prevalence (children aged 7)	57.9/10,000 for all ASDs 30.8/10,000 for AD	
2000	Center for Disease Control[19]	Prevalence investigation	Prevalence (children aged 3–10)	67/10,000 for all ASDs 40/10,000 for AD	
2001	Chakrabati & Fombonne[20]	Survey	Prevalence (children aged 2.5–6.5)	62.6/10,000 for all ASDs 16.8/10,000 for AD 45.8/10,000 for other ASDs including AS	

2.11 Divergent views were expressed in considering whether there has been a *real* rise, over time, in the prevalence of autism. Some of the submissions presented to the Expert Group attributed the increase to MMR. Most supported the conclusion that several factors, taken together, for example changing diagnostic thresholds, better and more active case ascertainment, survival, population flows, and changes in the prevalence of causal factors, may only have fuelled an *apparent* increase (i.e. the level of ASD is the same as it always was, but we have become better at recognising it).

2.12 The Expert Group endorses the conclusions reached by the MRC[8] and PHIS[9]:

- ASDs are considerably more common than has previously been recognised, with as many as 60 in 10,000 children affected.

- Whether there is a real rise in numbers is unclear.

Methodological differences between studies, changes in diagnostic practice and public and professional awareness are likely causes of apparent increases in prevalence. Whether these factors are sufficient to account for increased numbers of identified individuals, or whether there has been a rise in actual numbers affected, is as yet unclear.

2.13 What is clear is that "the full range of ASDs affect a very significant number of children"[8]. The PHIS report estimates that there are 7714 children under 19 with ASD in Scotland, and recognises that the prevalence of ASD among the adult population is not known. As such, there is now, perhaps, a more clearly defined gap between the recognised prevalence of ASD and the information previously used to plan related service provision. The importance of improving the educational, social and health services provided to individuals with ASD is addressed in paragraphs 2.43 to 2.51.

2.14 The perception that the rise in numbers may represent a real increase in ASD also drives the need for more research into causes, which is addressed in the following section.

The Causes of ASD

2.15 The report of the *MRC Review of Autism Research* gives a useful summary of the present available evidence relating to possible cause or causes of ASD. A cause can be defined as factor or exposure, which acts either alone or in conjunction with other factors to initiate a sequence of events, which may result in an effect.

2.16 It is important to restate that most diseases or disorders are rarely caused by a single agent, and may depend on a number of factors[7, 8, 21], which may be grouped together under three main headings:

- Agent – a disease may be caused by a microorganism or a chemical or physical agent, or the presence or absence of a particular dietary substance.

- Host – individual factors such as a person's genetic makeup or their nutritional status.

- Environment – this includes not only the physical environment a person is exposed to, for example the water they drink, chemicals and biological agents they might be exposed to but also the educational, occupational, economic and social status of the family or situation they live in.

The MRC Review confirms that most researchers support the view that ASDs have a variety of causes which, acting together, cause the disorder. These are discussed in the following paragraphs, and summarised in the opposite box.

2.17 This report has already summarised the criteria used to infer a causal association between risk factors and disorders. The aim of the research into ASD is to identify any causal associations, which should then assist the development of effective and appropriate interventions. The interventions must either prevent the disorder occurring or if established, help to manage the disorder and prevent complications.

Evidence of genetic causes for ASDs

2.18 Complex genetic influences contribute to the majority of ASD cases. Single gene or chromosome disorders may affect a small minority (perhaps 5–10%) of those with ASDs, for example: individuals with fragile X syndrome; phenylketonuria; Turner's syndrome; and tuberous sclerosis. Twin studies[23] have shown that ASDs are heritable: 60% of identical twins with ASD also have an ASD. These estimates are based on small numbers of twins ascertained using relatively narrowly defined criteria. The rate of ASD in other siblings is 2–6%[24], which is 10 times the prevalence in the general population.

2.19 Several genes may be operating together to confer susceptibility. The MRC Review suggests that chromosomes 2, 7, 16 and 17 offer the strongest possibility for identifying the genetic susceptibility loci for ASD. The MRC Review notes that some genes may only be associated with ASD and not necessarily causative and that genetic susceptibility may interact with environmental factors, which may lead to the expression of ASD. International collaborative groups are most likely to make best progress in the search for relevant genes.

Possible environmental risk factors for ASD

2.20 The MRC Review notes that a variety of possible risk factors other than genetic susceptibility for ASD has been suggested, including exposures, before or after birth, to drugs, infections and heavy metals including mercury. Although there is evidence that mercury can have serious effects on the developing brain[25], there is no conclusive evidence that cases of ASD show high levels of mercury. There is insufficient evidence to date to allow firm conclusions to be drawn about any causal association.

2.21 There have been recent suggestions that early exposure to thiomersal, a preservative containing approximately 49% ethylmercury that has been used as a preservative in vaccines, may be implicated as a risk factor for ASD. It is important to note that there is no thiomersal in MMR vaccine. An assessment of the scientific literature on thiomersal included analyses of published and unpublished studies proposing an association with disorders such as ASD, and found them to be inconclusive. No evidence currently exists that proves a link between thiomersal-containing vaccines and ASD[8].

2.22 There is some inconsistent, non-specific evidence that suggests prenatal exposures and perinatal complications may be more common in individuals with ASD[8]. Taking account of that, the MRC Review states that "it appears that obstetric complications may be a consequence, rather than a cause, of a child's ASD". This relates to the large head size that is a feature of many children with ASD. No specific prenatal exposures have been established as contributory.

ASDs have a variety of causes

GENES

Several genes probably interact
- But they have yet to be identified
- Evidence strongest – for chromosomes 2, 7, 16 and 17
- Identifying these genes will transform the research agenda
- But a simple genetic test is very unlikely

Interest in broader phenotype
- Subtle patterns in relatives
- Clues to distinct causal pathways for the different facets

Future research
- How genes and environment interact during early development
- The links between genes – brain structure & function – psychology

OTHER RISK FACTORS

The evidence on other risk factors is insufficient

Available evidence does not support
- Obstetric complications
- Various viruses, including measles
- Heavy metals including mercury
- Dietary minerals

Largely speculative, lacking evidence/replication
- Drugs, sex hormones, carbon monoxide, lead
- Abnormal immune function, allergies

Inadequate/not properly controlled studies
- Intestinal inflammation ("autistic enterocolitis")
- Intestinal permeability changes
- Gluten and casein
- Abnormal gut flora (study under way)
- Abnormal sulphur metabolism
- Significance of co-morbidities including epilepsy

MRC 2002[22]

2.23 Certain drugs have been implicated in association with ASD. The strongest evidence exists for intrauterine exposure to thalidomide, which is a drug known to have produced gross developmental abnormalities when taken during early pregnancy. Thalidomide is no longer a licensed medicine, although it can still be supplied to individual patients for specialised use under the responsibility of the individual doctor prescribing it. The observation that ASD are more common in males than females implicates sex hormones in the development of autistic traits, although this is not supported by direct evidence. Speculation has concerned the possible association of carbon monoxide poisoning or chronic exposure in mothers with anatomical and functional disturbances in their offspring, but there is no evidence to support its association with ASD.

2.24 The MRC Review reports evidence that a small number of cases has been reported in which viral infection (cytomegalovirus, herpes simplex and congenital rubella infection) may have played a role. These cases were sporadic and rare and are unlikely causative associations in the majority of individuals with ASD.

MMR and ASD

2.25 The MRC Review specifically comments on the scientific weight attributable to the published work by Wakefield et al[26], which implied that MMR vaccine was a risk factor in ASD based on 12 individual cases. The MRC Review states that, at present, there is no evidence for inflammation or histological responses to infection in patients with ASD.

2.26 The MRC Review also refers to a number of other expert review groups, all of whom have analysed the published work:

- the American Medical Association;

- the Institute of Medicine, USA;

- the World Health Organization;

- the American Academy of Pediatrics;

- the Population and Public Health Branch of Health Canada;

- the Irish Department of Health and Children.

All these reviews concluded that a causal link between the MMR vaccine and "autistic colitis" and ASD was not proven and that the existing body of epidemiological evidence did not support this proposed link. The Expert Group has not reviewed all the evidence presented to the previous expert review groups.

2.27 This Group considers it is important to note that the suggested link between MMR vaccine and "autistic colitis" and ASD must, as the MRC and others have stated, remain "a theoretical possibility", largely because of the impossibility of proving a negative. Currently there are no epidemiological studies[8] that provide reliable evidence to assert the hypotheses of association between MMR and ASD. The MRC Review recognised the need for more research into the causes of autism, and the Expert Group supports this.

2.28 The MRC Review examined a number of UK studies looking at the relationships between MMR and ASD. In one study of 498 ASD cases[1], methods were used to investigate clustering of ASD within defined post-immunisation periods as well as to investigate potential effects of second dose of MMR. There was a steady increase in cases by year of birth with no sudden change in the time trend after the introduction of MMR immunisation. There was no difference in age at diagnosis between the individuals vaccinated before or after 18 months of age and those never vaccinated. There was no temporal association between onset of ASD within 1 or 2 years after immunisation with MMR. Developmental regression was not clustered in the months after immunisation. A separate analysis[1] of the incidence of ASD in relation to the timing of MMR concluded that there was no evidence of an association. A further epidemiological study by the same group was published in February 2002[27]. The study demonstrated that the proportion of children with developmental regression or bowel symptoms has not changed significantly during the 20 years since 1970. There was also no significant difference in rates of bowel problems or regression in children who received the MMR vaccine before onset of parental concern about development, compared to those who received only after such concern and those who had not received MMR vaccine. A possible association between non-specific bowel problems and regression in children with autism was seen, but this was unrelated to MMR vaccination. The authors conclude that these findings therefore "provide no support for an MMR associated 'new variant' form of autism associated with developmental regression and bowel problems, and further evidence against involvement of MMR vaccine in the initiation of autism".

2.29 The MRC Review also examined a number of international studies looking at the links between MMR and ASD. A study from California published in 2001[1] looked at a retrospective analysis of MMR immunisation coverage rates among children born in 1980–94. School immunisation records were reviewed to determine retrospectively the age at which they first received MMR immunisation. No correlation was found between the time trend of early childhood MMR immunisation rates and the time trend in numbers of children with ASD. For the cohort studied, a marked, sustained increase in ASD case numbers was noted, but changes in early childhood MMR immunisation coverage over the same time period were much smaller and of shorter duration. These data do not suggest an association between MMR immunisation among young children and an increase in ASD occurrence.

2.30 One Finnish study[28] often referred to in the medical literature examined gastro-intestinal symptoms reported prospectively as adverse events in relation to MMR vaccine. The authors subsequently traced those vaccinated children who developed gastrointestinal symptoms. The records of these subjects were examined to determine whether any of those children with gastrointestinal symptoms later developed ASD or other neurological signs or symptoms. No child had developed an ASD when followed up for 9–10 years after immunisation. However, this particular report did not examine the relation of MMR and ASD irrespective of gastrointestinal symptoms and does not therefore provide useful evidence on this particular point.

2.31 The Expert Group received an oral presentation by Mr Andrew Wakefield (then) of the Inflammatory Bowel Disease Study Group at the Royal Free Hospital and School of Medicine, and, as such, one of the leading proponents of the hypotheses linking MMR, "autistic colitis" and ASD. That presentation was based in part on published research, and in part on research which had yet to be peer-reviewed and published (and which was therefore to be treated as confidential). Mr Wakefield was clear, consistent with testimonies elsewhere[2] and in published papers, that his research does not provide scientific evidence of a causal link between MMR, "autistic colitis" and ASD. While a number of questions posed to him subsequently by the Expert Group remain unanswered, the unpublished material which underpinned Mr Wakefield's presentation is now in the public domain. *"Potential viral pathogenic mechanism for new variant inflammatory bowel disease"*[29] *"reports the association of new variant inflammatory bowel disease with the persistence of at least fragments of measles virus found within the follicular dendritic cells and lymphocytes of areas of lymphoid nodular hyperplasia"*[21]. The associated editorial commentary states that *"the data presented here are unquestionably interesting but beg a string of further questions … we look forward to the answers"*[21].

2.32 The Expert Group also notes that both the editors of the journal in which the paper was published, and one of the co-authors, have stated that the study did not set out to investigate the role of MMR in the development of either bowel disease or developmental disorder, and no conclusions about such a role could, or should be, drawn from the findings.

Causation is rarely simple and never pure: most, if not all diseases are multifactorial in nature[8, 21].

Physiological abnormalities in ASD

2.33 There are a number of published studies that report gastrointestinal abnormalities in people with ASD including those that have received MMR vaccine (see for instance Akobeng and Thomas 1999; Horvath *et al* 1999; Wakefield *et al* 2000; Taylor *et al* 2002; Fombonne and Chakrabarti 2001[30]). It is not known whether or not these are exclusive to, or more common than, among non-ASD individuals with comparable dietary and bowel habits. The Expert Group acknowledges that association is not the same as causation, as has been discussed in paragraphs 1.26–1.31. The Expert Group was not tasked to evaluate technical scientific evidence and has relied on the reports of expert groups, in particular the *MRC Review of Autism Research* (2001), paragraphs 130–146[8]. Clearly further research in this area is needed.

2.34 Impaired sulphur metabolism has been reported for individuals with ASD using an indirect assay method. The finding is also noted in cases of rheumatoid arthritis, Parkinson's disease and motor neurone disease. This finding needs to be independently checked and replicated, preferably using a more direct method. Sulphur is important in the detoxification of certain substances in the body.

2.35 There is no clear pattern of differences in the immune system between children with ASD and those without. The MRC Review concluded that while there is considerable interest in possible immune problems in ASD, there is a lack of published research in this area, and as such there is no convincing evidence as to causal relationship between defects of the immune system and ASD.

2.36 Many ASD children are being offered certain exclusion diets such as casein and gluten-free diets with some reports of improvements. Data are presently limited, and further research, including appropriate control groups, would be of value. Anecdotal reports of the benefits of fish oil supplements have also been mentioned in research findings, but to date are inconclusive. The Expert Group is aware a large-scale study is underway examining the gut flora of children with ASD, and its findings are awaited with interest.

2.37 Brain abnormalities have been noted in some individuals with ASD. Brain weight is increased in a proportion of ASD cases, certain types of brain cells are decreased in the majority of cases studied, and some reports of developmental abnormalities are also reported. There is evidence that ASD is associated with abnormal cortical organisation, but more evidence and replication of findings are needed.

Research into the causes of ASD

2.38 The MRC Review of current research knowledge referred to the importance of broadening the future research agenda, in part because the focus has been centred on MMR. Conversely, we may know more about that issue than any other alleged environmental risk factor, because the specific question of the potential link between MMR immunisation and ASD has been the subject of extensive research.

2.39 The MRC Review also highlighted an extract from the Institute of Medicine report, which stated that *"more extensive research would be necessary to provide evidence for the biological plausibility of a suggested causal link between viral infections and ASD, as it would be for other proposed causal factors"*.

2.40 The Expert Group welcomes the MRC's plans to work with the research community to develop high quality research proposals for funding which address key issues for research, in particular, case-definition, the roles and interplay between genetic and environmental risk factors, causal pathways and mechanisms, and new approaches to treatment and perhaps prevention. **The Expert Group considers that The Scottish Executive and the Medical Research Council should work together to drive forward and fund, as appropriate, the full research agenda outlined in the final chapter of the MRC Review of Autism Research, which was informed by the concerns of parents and consumers. Parents and other representatives of those with autism must continue to play a key role in developing research strategies.**

2.41 The Expert Group also recommends that the Executive and the MRC should, in pursuing that research agenda, seek to maximise international collaboration.

2.42 The Expert Group recognises that, at any given time, governments, organisations and individuals base decisions on the body of scientific evidence that is then available. The Expert Group acknowledges, like the HCCC, the MRC and others, that on the basis of currently available evidence, there is no proven scientific link between the MMR vaccine and autism.

Diagnosis

Autism Spectrum Disorders (ASD) are diagnosed on the basis of qualitative abnormalities in social, communicative and imaginative behaviours, and the presence of repetitive and stereotyped patterns of interests and activities. Diagnosis is complicated by the varied manifestation of these core deficits, by wide variation in ability level, and by developmental changes.

MRC Review of Autism Research

2.43 ASD are typically characterised by a "triad of impairments"[31]:

- Social – impaired, deviant and extremely delayed social development, especially interpersonal development. The variation may be from "autistic aloofness" to "active but odd" characteristics.

- Language and communication – impaired and deviant language and communication, verbal and non-verbal. Deviant, semantic and pragmatic aspects of language.

- Thought and behaviour – rigidity of thought and behaviour and impoverished social imagination. Ritualistic behaviour, reliance on routines, extreme delay or absence of "pretend play".

Manifestations may vary for a number of reasons, including the presence of additional disorders, and changes in the way the disorder presents itself, or is perceived, at different ages or stages of development.

2.44 This "triad" of impairments is captured in current international classification systems (the World Health Organization's "International Classification of Diseases", 10th edition (ICD-10)[10] and the American Psychiatric Association's "Diagnostic and Statistical Manual", 4th edition (DSM-IV)[11]).

2.45 The MRC Review of Autism rightly acknowledged that "even in the presence of agreed broad diagnostic criteria for ASD, the methods by which information has been obtained… have varied". Evidence presented to the Expert Group supports the conclusion that diagnosis remains, for many, time-consuming and traumatic, and that generally, health, social care, and education professionals who do not specialise in ASD need up-to-date information and knowledge.

Diagnostic Criteria for Childhood Autism

International Classification of Diseases (ICD-10)

A   ABNORMAL OR IMPAIRED DEVELOPMENT IS EVIDENT BEFORE THE AGE OF 3 YEARS IN AT LEAST ONE OF THE FOLLOWING AREAS:

(1)   receptive or expressive language as used in social communication;

(2)   the development of selective social attachments or reciprocal social interaction;

(3)   functional or symbolic play.

B   A TOTAL OF AT LEAST SIX SYMPTOMS FROM (1), (2) AND (3) MUST BE PRESENT, WITH AT LEAST TWO FROM (1) AND AT LEAST ONE FROM EACH OF (2) AND (3):

(1)   *Qualitative abnormalities in reciprocal social interaction are manifest in at least two of the following areas:*

(a)   failure adequately to use eye-to-eye gaze, facial expression, body posture, and gesture to regulate social interaction;

(b)   failure to develop (in a manner appropriate to mental age, and despite ample opportunities) peer relationships that involve a mutual sharing of interests, activities and emotions;

(c)   lack of socio-emotional reciprocity as shown by an impaired or deviant response to other people's emotions; or lack of modulation of behaviour according to social context; or a weak integration of social, emotional and communicative behaviours;

(d)   lack of spontaneous seeking to share enjoyment, interests or achievements with other people (e.g. a lack of showing, bringing or pointing out to other people objects of interest to the individual).

(2)   *Qualitative abnormalities in communication are manifest in at least one of the following areas:*

(a)   a delay in, or total lack of, development of spoken language that is not accompanied by an attempt to compensate through the use of gesture or mime as an alternative mode of communication (often preceded by a lack of communicative babbling);

(b)   relative failure to initiate or sustain conversational interchange (at whatever level of language skills is present), in which there is reciprocal responsiveness to the communications of the other person;

(c)   stereotyped and repetitive use of language or idiosyncratic use of words or phrases;

(d)   lack of varied spontaneous make-believe or (when young) social imitative play.

(3)   *Restricted, repetitive, and stereotyped patterns of behaviour, interests, and activities are manifest in at least one of the following areas:*

(a)   an encompassing preoccupation with one or more stereotyped and restricted patterns of interest that are abnormal in content or focus; or one or more interests that are abnormal in their intensity and circumscribed nature though not in their content or focus;

(b)   apparently compulsive adherence to specific, non-functional routines or rituals;

(c)   stereotyped and repetitive motor mannerisms that involve either hand or finger flapping or twisting, or complex whole body movements;

(d)   preoccupations with part-objects or non-functioning elements of play materials (such as their odour, the feel of their surface, or the noise or vibration that they generate).

C   THE CLINICAL PICTURE IS NOT ATTRIBUTABLE TO THE OTHER VARIETIES OF PERVASIVE DEVELOPMENTAL DISORDER.

2.46 The Expert Group welcomes the (UK) National Initiative on Autism: Screening and Assessment (NIASA), which has been established by the Royal College of Paediatrics and Child Health and the Faculty of Child and Adolescent Psychiatry, Royal College of Psychiatrists, with the support of the National Autistic Society (NAS) and the All-Party Parliamentary Group on Autism (APPGA). A working group will begin to develop working guidelines and protocols for timely diagnosis.

Services

2.47 Based on evidence presented, the Expert Group was surprised and concerned by the apparent shortfall in the numbers of social and health professionals qualified and resourced to both diagnose ASD and provide appropriate support and assistance thereafter. The Group also noted the scope for improvements in inter-agency working. The Expert Group strongly endorses the views of the Public Health Institute of Scotland (PHIS) Needs Assessment Report[9]:

"Current service provision is patchy and inadequate for the numbers of individuals with ASD requiring support:

- *Health care, education and social services vary depending on local resources and there are marked differences in ease of access to services due to limited facilities in some geographical areas.*
- *Although there are examples of good, innovative and multi-agency practice across Scotland, there are some areas and some client groups, particularly adults and their families, who experience long delays and inconsistencies in the delivery of services and very little support after diagnosis. The transition from child to adult services is particularly problematic."*

"Services should aim to deliver:

- *Joint assessment, delivery and review of care in a way that involves the relevant agencies, services and skilled and experienced professionals.*
- *Active involvement of the family and the individual with ASD.*
- *Early identification.*
- *Appropriate early interventions.*
- *Provision of a range of services delivered seamlessly to meet the various and differing needs of people with ASD, that are client centred and are planned and developed in a truly multi-agency and seamless way.*
- *Well planned and sensitive management of the transition between childhood and adulthood within and between agencies.*
- *All planning carried out should place the person at the centre of services and ensure that individual needs are addressed.*
- *Joint policies, strategies and operational arrangements between agencies."*

2.48 The Expert Group considers the last of these to be particularly important and recognises the precedent established by *Report of the Joint Futures Group (Community Care)*[32]. **The Group recommends that all agencies working with those with ASD (and their families) develop joint policies, strategies and operational arrangements**

based on that model. However, the Expert Group considers it vitally important that representatives of the "users" or "consumers" of those services should be part of that ongoing management process, in a way that did not take place in the context of community care.

2.49 The Expert Group also looks to The Scottish Executive to consult widely, in order to publish a firm timetable for addressing all of the detailed recommendations set out in the *PHIS Autistic Spectrum Disorders Needs Assessment Report*, and in particular those relating to improved diagnosis and management of ASD, the need for a more coherent and systematic approach to training health, education and social care professionals, better and in appropriate numbers <u>and</u> developing and maintaining a database of people with ASD in Scotland. The Expert Group recognises that additional funding will be required as a consequence.

2.50 The Expert Group acknowledges that the Scottish Special Need System and the mapping exercise currently being undertaken by the Scottish Society for Autism may inform and underpin that work considerably.

2.51 The Expert Group also acknowledges that similar views and concerns might be expressed in relation to other conditions, falling outwith its remit. However, there is now, perhaps, a more clearly defined gap between the recognised prevalence of autism, and the information previously used to plan future service provision. It may be that, in the longer term, the resultant standard of integrated educational, health and social care provided to those with ASD will become the benchmark against which service provision is assessed.

Chapter 2 – Summary of Key Points

ASD is a set of neurodevelopmental disorders which impair a person's capacity to communicate and interact with others. It is a complex, debilitating and lifelong condition.

The MRC Review of Autism Research (December 2001) represents the most up-to-date expert assessment of the range and relative merit of current research evidence. As such, the Expert Group endorses the conclusions reached by the MRC:

- ASD is considerably more common than has previously been recognised; methodological differences between studies, changes in diagnostic practice and public and professional awareness are likely causes of this increase in prevalence.

- Current research evidence indicates that ASD have many possible genetic and environmental risk factors which, acting together, may cause the disorder; on the basis of currently available evidence, there is no proven scientific link between the MMR vaccine and autism.

- Key issues for future research include case-definition, the roles and interplay between genetic and environmental risk factors, causal pathways and mechanisms, and new approaches to treatment.

The Expert Group has recommended more research and significantly better services.

3 Crohn's Disease

This chapter describes:

- Inflammatory Bowel Disease (IBD) (paragraphs 3.3 to 3.6);

- how common IBD is, based on current evidence (paragraphs 3.7 to 3.9); and

- what we know, at present, about the causes of IBD (paragraphs 3.10 to 3.16).

Introduction

3.1 Earlier chapters have touched upon the way in which inflammatory bowel disease (IBD) and intestinal abnormalities have been considered in the context of people with ASD.

3.2 This chapter focuses on Crohn's disease and IBD more generally, taking account of the issues raised by the Health and Community Care Committee, and recognising that it is a serious and debilitating condition in its own right.

Crohn's Disease

3.3 Crohn's disease is a form of inflammatory bowel disease. It is a chronic condition, in which the intestines become swollen, inflamed and ulcerated. Symptoms can include pain in the abdomen, loss of weight, diarrhoea, anaemia, tiredness and lack of energy. Some patients also have swollen joints, inflamed eyes or skin rashes.

3.4 Most patients experience intermittent and unpredictable flare-ups of symptoms with periods of better health in-between. Treatment with drugs or surgery can control or reduce most of the symptoms, but many people find that their general well-being and daily activities are affected to some extent, even when the condition is not active. There is no cure for the condition at present.

3.5 There is another form of inflammatory bowel disease called ulcerative colitis which has some similar symptoms, but which affects only the large bowel.

3.6 Neither Crohn's disease nor ulcerative colitis is thought to be infectious.

Prevalence and Incidence

3.7   It is estimated that within Northern Europe about 0.5% of the population has chronic inflammatory bowel disease[33] and the same figure probably applies to the UK.

3.8   The British Paediatric Surveillance Unit (BPSU) reported the incidence of IBD in the British Isles to be 0.52 per 10,000 per year in young people aged less than 16 years. The highest UK regional incidence was Scotland with a rate of 0.65 per 10,000 per year[34].

3.9   Scotland is fortunate in having data on the incidence and prevalence of childhood IBD extending back more than 30 years. The incidence of Crohn's disease in young people in Scotland rose four-fold between 1968 and 1992 from 0.07 to 0.29 per 10,000 per year[35]. The most recent estimate of the prevalence of Crohn's disease in children aged less than 16 years is 1.37 cases per 10,000 population in Scotland[36].

The Causes of Crohn's Disease

3.10   It is not known what causes Crohn's disease. Epidemiological data, notably concordance rates in siblings and in twin pairs, have emphasised the importance of both environmental and genetic factors in disease pathogenesis. It has been known for a long time that some families are more likely to suffer from inflammatory bowel disease than others, and recent research has identified particular genes that are found more often in people who have Crohn's disease[37]. NOD-2/CARD15 has been identified as an "IBD1 gene" by independent groups in Chicago[38] and Paris[39], and these data have been confirmed in German and British adult populations[40].

3.11   Which precise environmental factors trigger the onset of Crohn's disease are not known. At different times, research has focused on, for example, viruses, deficiencies in the body's immune system, hereditary factors, mycobacteria in water or milk, diet (including breast-feeding in infancy) and lifestyle (including smoking). No single factor has yet been identified as the most likely agent. Stress, which was sometimes thought to be a primary cause in the 1940s and 1950s, is now accepted to be a factor, which may at times make symptoms worse, but does not cause the illness.

3.12   The measles virus is one of the possible environmental triggers suggested as causing Crohn's disease, based on laboratory and epidemiological studies. The Inflammatory Bowel Disease Study Group at the Royal Free Hospital, London, claimed to identify virus particles in the parts of the bowel damaged by Crohn's disease, which it believed to be evidence of measles infection. It is known that the measles virus can persist within the body long after a measles infection, as occurs, for example, in subacute sclerosing panencephalitis (SSPE), a rare late effect of measles. The Royal Free researchers suggested that the measles virus damages the blood vessels supplying the intestine and that this leads to the damage and symptoms characteristic of Crohn's disease[41]. However, other separate groups of researchers have since reported that they cannot find measles virus in tissue affected by Crohn's disease[42]. The Royal Free research group has also repeated its original work using more sensitive tests and has been unable to detect measles virus[43].

3.13 Since the publication some years ago of Swedish and UK epidemiological surveys suggesting a link between measles virus, vaccine and Crohn's disease[44], most published research from the UK and elsewhere has reported no evidence of any such link[45].

3.14 The possible connection between MMR vaccine, bowel disease and autism was raised first by the Royal Free Hospital researchers, in a report published in the *Lancet*[46]. This article and later publications[47] have been reviewed by a number of expert groups[2]. While there may be abnormalities of the bowel in some children with ASD, it is not proven that they are either a feature of, or involved in, the pathogenesis of ASD. Moreover they are not the same as those found in childhood Crohn's disease.

3.15 It is, of course, important that all this research is carried forward in an effort to learn more and more about Crohn's disease. The Expert Group welcomes plans to undertake more epidemiological research of, and investigation of, environmental risk factors for early onset of IBD in Scotland which will:

• Help to define the natural history of IBD in childhood.

• Obtain data on early onset incidence for 10% of the UK population.

• Undertake genetic and environmental studies in a large and clearly defined population.

3.16 The Expert Group recommends that The Scottish Executive and the Medical Research Council should work together to drive forward and fund, as appropriate, that research into inflammatory bowel disease in children.

Chapter 3 – Summary of Key Points

Crohn's disease is a form of inflammatory bowel disease. It is a chronic condition, for which there is no cure at present.

The most recent estimate of the prevalence of Crohn's disease in children aged less than 16 years is 1.37 cases per 10,000 population in Scotland.

We do not know what causes Crohn's disease. Epidemiological data have emphasised the importance of both environmental and genetic factors. Which precise environmental factors trigger the onset of Crohn's disease are not known. Some researchers have suggested a possible connection between MMR vaccine, bowel disease and autism. All relevant research has been reviewed by a number of expert groups, and, while there may be abnormalities of the bowel in some children with ASD, the scientific evidence does not support the conclusion that they are either a feature of, or involved in, the pathogenesis of ASD.

The Expert Group has recommended more research into inflammatory bowel disease in children.

4 Vaccine Testing and Monitoring

This chapter describes:

- the roles and responsibilities of the Joint Committee on Vaccination and Immunisation, the Committee on Safety of Medicines and the Medicines Control Agency (paragraphs 4.1 to 4.6);

- How vaccines are tested, and the monitoring of adverse effects (paragraphs 4.7 to 4.18);

- the licensing of MMR vaccines (paragraphs 4.19 to 4.25); and

- the scope for importing unlicensed products (paragraphs 4.26 to 4.29) and how that relates to measles and mumps vaccines (paragraphs 4.30 to 4.35).

Introduction

4.1 The Expert Group was asked to describe the process of vaccine testing and the monitoring of adverse effects, having regard to the role and remit of the Joint Committee on Vaccination and Immunisation (JCVI), the Committee on Safety of Medicines (CSM) and the Medicines Control Agency (MCA).

4.2 The Joint Committee on Vaccination and Immunisation is a statutory expert Standing Advisory Committee established in England and Wales under the National Health Service Act 1977. The Committee has no statutory basis in Scotland or Northern Ireland, but fulfils the same role and has the same responsibilities. The Committee has no executive function. Its terms of reference are:

> "To advise the Secretary of State for Health, the Scottish Ministers, the Northern Ireland Ministers responsible for health and the National Assembly for Wales on matters relating to communicable diseases, preventable and potentially preventable through immunisation."

The Committee as a whole has a responsibility to provide high quality and considered advice and recommendations to Ministers on the matters set out in its terms of reference. This includes giving advice and recommendations on matters of both a "routine" nature and also on any specific or special matters that Ministers may from time to time request. In formulating its advice and recommendations, the Committee must take into account the need for and impact of vaccines, the quality of vaccines and their safety and the strategies to ensure that the greatest benefit to the public health can be obtained from the most appropriate use of vaccines. Members are expected to make a full and considered contribution to this work.

4.3   The Committee on Safety of Medicines (CSM) is one of the independent advisory committees established under the Medicines Act. It advises the UK Licensing Authority (UK Health Ministers) on the quality, efficacy and safety of medicines in order to ensure that appropriate public health standards are met and maintained. The Committee members are appointed, for 3-year terms, by UK Health Ministers following a wide-ranging consultation process. There are two lay members. The Committee's responsibilities are, broadly, two-fold:

- To give advice with respect to safety, quality and efficacy in relation to human use of any substance or article (not being an instrument, apparatus or appliance) to which any provision of the Medicines Act 1968 is applicable.

- To promote the collection and investigation of information relating to adverse reactions for the purpose of enabling such advice to be given.

Summaries of the minutes of all meetings of Committee are published on the MCA website.

4.4   The UK Medicines Control Agency (MCA) is the executive arm of the UK Licensing Authority. It is an Executive Agency of the Department of Health. Its primary objective is to safeguard public health by ensuring that all medicines on the UK market meet appropriate standards of safety, quality and efficacy. Safety aspects cover potential or actual harmful effects; quality relates to development and manufacture; and efficacy is a measure of the beneficial effect of the medicine on patients.

4.5   The Agency achieves that objective through:

- a system of licensing before the marketing of medicines;

- monitoring of medicines and acting on safety concerns after they have been placed on the market;

- variation and renewal of marketing authorisations and reclassification of legal status;

- inspecting standards of pharmaceutical manufacture and wholesaling;

- enforcement of medicines legislation;

- regulation of product information and advertising.

4.6   The Expert Group acknowledges the help and support provided by all those organisations in collating the material that follows.

A Summary of the Process of Vaccine Testing and the Monitoring of Adverse Effects

4.7   The control of medicines in the UK is primarily through the system of licensing laid down in EC legislation, in the Medicines Act (1968), and in relevant subordinate legislation. This legislation covers, among other things, the systems by which licences to manufacture, market, distribute, sell and supply medicinal products are granted by Ministers or, in the new centralised licensing system, by the relevant Community institutions.

4.8 The MCA operates a system of licensing before the marketing of medicines. Medicines which meet the standards of safety, quality and efficacy are granted a marketing authorisation (previously a product licence), which is normally necessary before they can be prescribed or sold. This authorisation covers all the main activities associated with the marketing of a medicinal product. The MCA carries out pre-marketing assessment of the medicine's safety, quality and efficacy, examining all the research and test results in detail, before a decision is made on whether the product should be granted a marketing authorisation.

4.9 Before a product is marketed, experience of its safety and efficacy is limited to its use in clinical trials. The conditions under which patients are studied pre-marketing do not necessarily reflect the way the medicine will be used in hospital or in general practice once it is marketed. Consequently, there is a continued need for vigilance to detect adverse effects that become apparent after marketing and when the medicine is more widely used among a greater variety of patients.

4.10 "Pharmacovigilance" is the process of:

(a) monitoring medicines as used in everyday practice to identify previously unrecognised or changes in the patterns of their adverse effects;

(b) assessing the risks and taking account of the benefits of medicines in order to determine what action, if any, is necessary to improve their safe use;

(c) providing information to users to optimise safe and effective use of medicines; and

(d) monitoring the impact of any action taken.

4.11 "Pharmacovigilance" uses many different sources of information including spontaneous adverse drug reaction (ADR) reporting schemes, clinical and epidemiological studies, the world literature, morbidity and mortality databases. The MCA and the Committee on Safety of Medicines are responsible for the UK's spontaneous adverse drug reaction reporting scheme (called the 'Yellow Card' reporting scheme) to which doctors, dentists, pharmacists and coroners/procurators fiscal report suspected adverse drug reactions. Health professionals are requested to report only serious[III] suspected adverse reactions for established medicines, whereas it is requested that ALL suspected adverse drug reactions are reported for the newer "Black Triangle" medicines. In addition, health professionals are strongly encouraged to report ALL suspected ADRs that have occurred in children whether associated with a "Black Triangle" or established medicine. The scheme provides an important early warning of suspected adverse reactions to medicines by collating information required to assess the association between the suspected adverse reaction and the medicine. This scheme may identify previously unknown side-effects or indicate that certain known side-effects occur more commonly than previously believed. It may also identify at-risk groups of patients for particular adverse reactions. Such findings can lead to changes in the marketing authorisation, for example restrictions in use, refinement of dose instructions or the introduction of specific warnings of side-effects in product information, which allow medicines to be used more safely and effectively.

[III] Serious reactions include those that are fatal, life-threatening, disabling, incapacitating or which result in or prolong hospitalisation and/or are medically significant. Other reactions that are considered serious include congenital abnormalities. Examples of reactions which are medically significant are given on the Committee on Safety of Medicines website.

4.12 When a hazard is considered unacceptable, a medicine may have to be withdrawn from the market. When drugs are removed from the market, action is usually taken voluntarily by pharmaceutical companies, but there are powers for the licensing authority to compulsorily vary, revoke or suspend marketing authorisations.

4.13 A European system for drug regulation was introduced in January 1995. There are three systems for licensing medicines in Europe: the centralised system by which a single EU licence is granted; a mutual recognition procedure whereby a licence in one Member State is recognised by others, and a national procedure for medicines licensed in only one Member State.

> *The main value of spontaneous reporting schemes, like the Yellow Card Scheme, is in the early detection of previously unrecognised possible drug safety hazards. It is recognised that the Yellow Card Scheme is particularly useful for identifying rare adverse drug effects, especially disorders that do not have a high background incidence and which occur in close temporal association to administration of the drug. The Yellow Card Scheme is recognised to be one of the best spontaneous reporting schemes in the world in terms of the level of reporting and has a proven track record of identifying new drug safety hazards. Although spontaneous reports are useful in signal detection, there are often limitations to their use in signal evaluation. While spontaneous reporting systems serve to generate hypotheses, drug safety signals often need to be further investigated by other methods, such as epidemiological studies, to confirm and quantify any risk.*
>
> *Medicines Control Agency*

4.14 The Committee for Proprietary Medicinal Products (CPMP) is the advisory body which advises on matters relating to medicines in the EU. The Pharmacovigilance Working Party is a working party of the CPMP with representation from all Member States, which provides a forum for reaching consensus on drug safety issues and for promoting the development of common pharmacovigilance practices. The MCA takes a leading role in European Pharmacovigilance. As laid down in European Community legislation, the regulatory authorities of the European Member States exchange information and work closely together on drug safety matters.

4.15 The work of the MCA in pharmacovigilance is conducted in a world-wide context, with close links and increasing information transfer with other regulatory authorities, for example the Food and Drug Administration (FDA) in the USA.

4.16 The MCA, like any other medicines regulator, does not routinely, proactively encourage companies to seek licences for products. The Expert Group notes that, in this sense, regulatory authorities in medicines cannot be compared directly with conventional regulators, for example, the Office for the Regulation of Electricity and Gas (OFREG), in terms of powers, roles and responsibilities. The responsibility for bringing a medicinal product to the market, and collating the necessary evidence to support licensure rests with the manufacturer. It is therefore vitally important that the MCA licensing process remains, rigorous and demanding. The Expert Group acknowledges that the MCA operates within a very robust system of medicine legislation, which is largely European, and therefore applies equally to all Member States.

4.17 Some submissions presented to the Expert Group raised questions about the value of the Yellow Card reporting scheme. While acknowledging the main strengths of the Yellow Card system, the data are not expected to serve an important role in substantiating or eliminating concerns about potential contributory long-term effects of immunisation. The Expert Group recognised that the use of the scheme for detection is limited when, under near-universal application of immunisation, there are potential difficulties in a health care professional attributing suspicion to gradual or delayed changes in a patient.

4.18 The Expert Group considers it important that the Medicines Control Agency should continue to work closely with the European Union, and appropriate corresponding bodies in individual Member States, to improve collaboration and monitoring of vaccine safety issues. The Expert Group also recommends that the MCA should regularly review the operation, management and voluntary nature of the 'Yellow Card' system in the light of such developments.

The Licensing of MMR Vaccines

4.19 A combined measles, mumps and rubella vaccine (MMR-I) was first licensed in the UK in 1972, but it was not actually used then, because combined measles, mumps and rubella vaccines were not introduced into the UK routine childhood immunisation programme until 1988, by which time MMR-II had replaced MMR-I (differing in the rubella virus strain only), and other similar combination vaccines had been licensed. Prior to 1988, the safety of measles, mumps and rubella combination vaccines was well established based on their world-wide use (over 500 million doses of MMR have been given since the mid-1970s); such vaccines had been routinely used in the USA since the early 1970s and in Scandinavia since 1982. Initially, a single dose was given, but a two-dose immunisation schedule with measles, mumps and rubella vaccine has existed in the UK since October 1996 (the first dose is given at 12–15 months and the second dose at 3–5 years).

Components/strains of MMR used since 1988:

From 1988 to present:
MMR II *(Ender's Edmonston (measles), Wistar RA27/3 (rubella) and Jeryl Lynn (mumps) strains)*

From 1998 to present:
Priorix *(Schwarz (measles), Wistar RA27/3 (rubella) and RIT438 (derived from Jeryl Lynn (mumps) strains)*

From 1988/89 to September 1992 (no longer used due to presence of Urabe mumps strain):

Pluserix (licence now cancelled) **and Immravax** *(Schwarz (measles), Wistar RA27/3 (rubella) and Urabe Am 9 (mumps) strains)*

4.20 Five combined measles, mumps and rubella vaccines have been licensed in the UK (including MMR-I). Three of these are still licensed and two (MMR II – Pasteur Merieux MSD and Priorix – GSK Biologicals) are routinely used in the national immunisation programme. Following the introduction of combined measles, mumps and rubella vaccine in 1988, sporadic case reports in the literature of mumps virus meningitis were reported in association with vaccines containing the Urabe Am 9 strain of mumps. Fewer cases were reported in association with combined measles, mumps and rubella vaccines containing the Jeryl Lynn strain. Since the Jeryl Lynn strain appeared to carry a lower risk of meningitis and meningo-encephalitis, only combined measles, mumps and rubella vaccines containing this strain were made available from 1992 (no licensing action has been taken against those containing Urabe Am 9 as the Committee on Safety of Medicines (CSM) concluded that the balance of risks and benefits remained positive).

4.21 In accordance with the principles of good clinical practice, the majority of clinical trials that supported licensure of these five MMR vaccines, similarly to other medicinal products, were sponsored by the company, were conducted by investigators experienced in the field, and were monitored by company personnel. The licensing procedure for the MMR vaccines was not different to that adopted for other vaccines or, indeed, for any other medicinal product.

4.22 Most of the studies enrolled children in the second year of life, although some enrolled children up to 13 years old. Details of adverse reactions were mostly recorded over 4–6 weeks post-injection, because children returned for assessment of their immune response to the vaccines around this time. A minority of children was followed for longer. However, post-marketing reporting of adverse reactions by the marketing authorisation holders and published studies of vaccine safety provide much additional information on the safety of these products.

4.23 In January 2001, an article by Mr Wakefield and Dr Montgomery in the journal *Adverse Drug Reactions and Toxicological Reviews*[48] reviewed several papers which, the authors claimed, suggest that MMR vaccines are more harmful than the single component vaccines given separately and that MMR vaccine was licensed prematurely. These claims were thoroughly assessed, answered and rejected by CSM in January 2001[49].

4.24 The submissions presented to the Expert Group fully support the conclusion that MMR was appropriately and rigorously tested before introduction, consistent with standards and science relevant at the time. We note that the process has subsequently been formally reviewed by the MCA, who confirmed that licensing followed normal procedures, clinical trials met the satisfactory standards of the time and follow-up of patients was in accordance with usual practices on vaccine trials. The Expert Group also recognises that the MCA continually monitors the safety of MMR vaccines in clinical practice and, if necessary, updates the Marketing Authorisation and product information if and when new data become available. For example, the "signal" that idiopathic thrombocytopenic purpura (ITP) could be caused, very rarely, by vaccines has been examined. A recent publication[50] has shown that this signal is a genuine indication of a rare problem.

4.25 The Expert Group further recognised that the identification and analysis of conditions which appear to emerge some considerable time after the administration of any medicine, and which may or may not be connected, may require supporting epidemiological evidence.

Medicines Legislation and Policy: Unlicensed Products

4.26 The Medicines Act 1968 contains an exemption which allows the supply of unlicensed relevant medicinal products for human use (commonly known as "specials") in response to a genuine, unsolicited order, formulated in accordance with the specification of a doctor or dentist, and for use by his individual patients on the doctor's or dentist's direct personal responsibility. In the interest of public health the exemption is narrowly drawn, because these products, unlike licensed products, have not been assessed by the licensing authority against the criteria of safety, quality and efficacy.

4.27 Responsibility for deciding whether an individual patient has "special needs" which the licensed product cannot meet is a matter for the doctor responsible for the patient's care.

4.28 A medicinal product should be regarded as a "pharmaceutical equivalent" if:

- it contains the same amount of the same active substance(s, or in the case of liquid dosage forms the same concentration;

- it is in the same dosage form; and

- it meets the same or comparable standards considered in the light of the clinical needs of the patient at the time of use of the product.

4.29 These restrictions on the import of unlicensed medicines are needed because, as already established, the unlicensed medicines known as "specials" have not been assessed by the licensing authority against the criteria of safety, quality and efficacy. To protect public health, manufacturers and importers of unlicensed "specials" must hold licences for the purpose and comply with their licence conditions. Importers' licence conditions include the requirement that they must notify the MCA on each occasion that they intend to import an unlicensed "special". Importation may proceed unless the importer has been informed by the MCA within 28 days that it objects to importation. The MCA may object, and prevent importation, if it has concerns about the safety or quality of the product, or because there is an equivalent medicinal product available, and it is not satisfied that there is a "special need" for the supply to an individual patient.

Importation Policy Specific to Measles, Mumps and Rubella Vaccines

4.30 Combined MMR is the licensed medicine recommended for immunisation of children against measles, mumps and rubella. There are single component measles, mumps and rubella vaccines licensed in the UK. The licensed measles and mumps vaccines are not currently marketed by their licence holders in the UK. However, rubella vaccines are available in the UK, and are used mainly for the immunisation of women of child-bearing age who have been found to be non-immune either before or between pregnancies.

The Medicines (Standard Provisions for Licences and Certificates) Amendment Regulations 1999 (SI 1999/4)

Importation Process

Licence holder notifies Licensing Authority of his intention to import exempted products:

- In writing
- No later than 28 days prior to each importation.

⇩

Notification should state the following:

- Name of medicinal product
  [i.e. Brand name *or* common name, *or* scientific name]
- Trademark *or* name of manufacturer of product
- International non-proprietary name *or* British approved name *or* the monograph name of each active ingredient
  [Where this is not valid, the accepted scientific name]
- Quantity to be imported
  [Not exceeding 25 single administrations *or* 25 courses of treatment sufficient for a maximum of 3 months]
- Name and address of manufacturer *or* assembler of the product in the form it is to be imported *or* name and address of supplier.

⇩

Licensing Authority acknowledges the notification in writing.

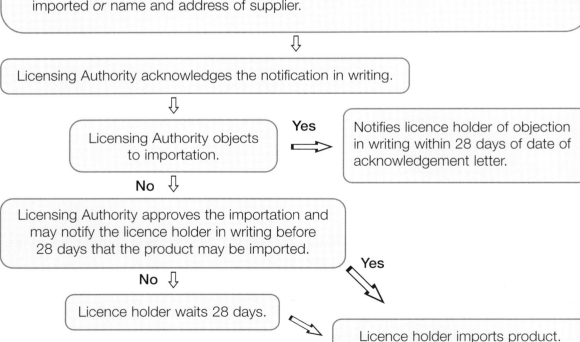

⇩

| Licensing Authority objects to importation. | **Yes** ⇨ | Notifies licence holder of objection in writing within 28 days of date of acknowledgement letter. |

No ⇩

Licensing Authority approves the importation and may notify the licence holder in writing before 28 days that the product may be imported.

Yes

No ⇩

Licence holder waits 28 days.

Licence holder imports product.

4.31 However, as set out above, existing legislation allows a licensed importer to import an unlicensed mono-component vaccine and supply it in response to a doctor's prescription to meet the "special needs" of an individual patient, on the doctor's direct personal responsibility. The process is summarised in the flow charts shown.

4.32 The Scottish Executive Health Department's Deputy Chief Medical Officer, Chief Nursing Officer and Chief Pharmaceutical Officer provided relevant guidance for all NHS health professionals in December 2000. A letter about the MMR vaccination programme stated that *"unlicensed medicines may be imported for use in private practice or the NHS… in accordance with the provisions of the Marketing Regulations"*.

4.33 The MCA has confirmed that the importation of unlicensed monocomponent vaccines is not uncommon. The figures for 2001 are shown below. These unlicensed vaccines have not been assessed by the MCA against the criteria of safety, quality and efficacy.

Data for total numbers of doses of unlicensed imported monocomponent measles and mumps vaccines notified to MCA-I&E in 2001 (UK)[IV]

Brand	Strain	Qty Imported (No. Doses)
Measles		
Attenuvax	Enders Edmonston	3480
Masern-Impfstoff Merieux	Schwarz	3525
Rimevax	Schwarz	75
Rouvax	Schwarz	1350
Moraten Berna ~ Vaccination	Edmonston-Zagreb strain	4625
Mumps		
Mumpsvax	Jeryl Lynn strain	24,022

4.34 The choice of strain(s) of virus in vaccines is part of the childhood vaccination programme. While specifications of vaccines derived from similar strains might be expected to be broadly equivalent, the purpose of licensing, in part, is to assure that equivalence through the specification of manufacture, storage and testing of the individual product.

[IV] Around 1.5 million doses of MMR are administered annually in the UK.

Importation Monitoring Process

Licence holder informs Licensing Authority that the safety or quality of the product is questionable.

The Licensing Authority investigates and decides the product is acceptable.

Yes

Licence holder continued to import or supply product.

 No

The Licensing Authority issues a written notice directing the licence holder that as from a given date the product or class of product may not be imported.

Licence holder ceases importation or supplying of product.

4.35 Taking all of that into account, the Expert Group considers that vaccination records relating to individual patients should always include details of the name and batch number of the vaccine administered. The Expert Group recommends that the Scottish Executive should:

- make this a standard requirement for vaccination records;

- progress the concept of a lifelong vaccination record which would allow identification of the immunisation status of an individual throughout the health service – irrespective of age group and independent of setting;

- require NHS Health Boards to put in place adequate quality assurance mechanisms to ensure accuracy and completeness of recording of vaccination data.

Chapter 4 – Summary of Key Points

MMR vaccines licensing followed normal procedure and was based on the provision of satisfactory data regarding safety and efficacy in adequate numbers of children. MMR vaccines were not licensed prematurely.

The safety of combined measles, mumps and rubella vaccines has been reviewed repeatedly by the Committee on Safety of Medicines and others. All of these expert groups have concluded that the evidence does not support an association between combined measles, mumps and rubella vaccines and inflammation of the bowel or autism. It is not that there is no evidence, but that the available evidence does not show an association.

UK legislation allows a licensed importer to import an unlicensed monocomponent vaccine and supply it in response to a doctor's prescription to meet the "special needs" of an individual patient, on the doctor's direct personal responsibility. Whether an individual patient has a "special need" which a licensed equivalent may not meet is a matter of clinical judgement by the prescriber.

The Expert Group has recommended that the MCA should continue to work closely with equivalent bodies across the world, and that, in Scotland, vaccination records relating to individual patients should always include details of the name and batch number of the vaccine administered.

5 The Consequences of Alternative Vaccination Policies

This chapter describes:

- the risks associated with measles, mumps and rubella (paragraphs 5.2 to 5.7);

- the purpose of vaccination, both generally and in relation to measles, mumps and rubella (paragraphs 5.8 to 5.12);

- the immunisation policy in place in Scotland and the UK, and elsewhere in Europe (paragraphs 5.13 to 5.25);

- a framework of principles for immunisation policy (paragraph 5.26 to 5.31); and

- the possible consequences of alternative vaccination policies (paragraphs 5.32 to 5.52).

Introduction

5.1 As indicated in paragraph 1.7, the Expert Group was asked by the Executive to describe the consequences of pursuing an alternative vaccination policy to MMR, and as such recognised that it was not expected or required to review MMR policy or the current immunisation programme. The Group also acknowledged that the Health and Community Care Committee's 8th Report stated that:

"The Committee believes that on the basis of currently available evidence, there is no proven scientific link between the measles, mumps and rubella (MMR) vaccine and autism or Crohn's disease and therefore the Committee has no reason to doubt the safety of the MMR vaccine. The Committee does not recommend any change in the current immunisation programme at this time."

Other "matters raised by the Health and Community Care Committee" are largely defined by a series of questions posed by the Committee, which broadly underpin the formal remit of the Expert Group. The questions and answers are set out in Chapter 6.

Risks Associated with Measles, Mumps and Rubella

5.2   The success of immunisation against measles, mumps and rubella has led to a decline in the incidence of these diseases. As a result, the serious risks[6] associated with measles, mumps and rubella infection may not be fully appreciated:

Complications of measles	Complications of mumps	Complications of rubella
• ear infection (1 in 20) • pneumonia/bronchitis (1 in 25) • convulsions (1 in 200) • diarrhoea (1 in 6) • meningitis/encephalitis (1 in 1000) • conditions affecting blood clotting (1 in 6000) • late onset subacute sclerosing panencephalitis (SSPE) (1 in 8000 children under 2 years) • deaths (1–2 deaths in 1000 reported cases in recent years)	• viral meningitis (1 in 20) • encephalitis (1 in 1000) • permanent hearing loss (1 in 20,000) • inflammation of testicles (4 in 10 adult males) • inflammation of ovaries	• encephalitis (1 in 6000) • birth defects (90% chance baby will have birth defects if mother catches rubella early in pregnancy). Birth defects include blindness, deafness, learning difficulties and heart disease • conditions affecting blood clotting (1 in 3000)

5.3   Serious complications have been reported for one in 15 notified cases of measles[51], but are more common and severe in chronically ill children[52]. A particularly distressing complication is subacute sclerosing panencephalitis (SSPE). This is a rare degenerative neurological condition that can develop some years after natural measles infection to cause gradual loss of function and death within a few years[53]. The risk is greatest in those who were infected at a young age. The graph below shows that the incidence of SSPE has decreased with the reduction in measles. Case fatality rates for measles infection, in general, are age related, and so rates vary depending on the age at infection. However, in recent years, one to two people in every 1000 with reported measles infection have died from it[54].

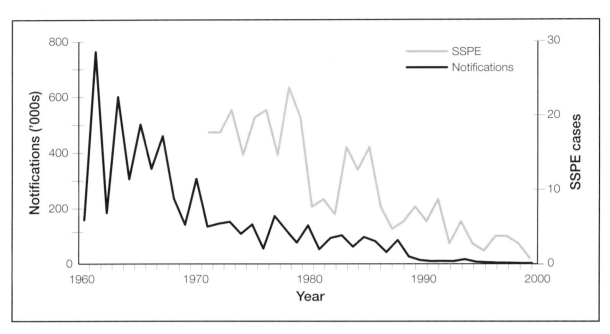

Source: PHLS-CDSC

5.4 Death from measles is highest in children under one year – a group that do not receive MMR vaccine – and in those who are immunosuppressed, due to disease (e.g. leukaemia) or treatment (e.g. organ transplantation) and cannot receive MMR vaccine (or indeed single vaccines). In children receiving immunosuppressive treatment, e.g. for leukaemia or after organ transplantation, measles was a major cause of morbidity and mortality. Between 1970 and 1983, 19 children with acute lymphatic leukaemia died from measles in England and Wales[54]. A study conducted at four UK hospitals between 1974 and 1984 identified 3 cases of measles encephalitis and two cases of measles pneumonia in children with acute lymphoblastic leukaemia at the Royal Hospitals for Sick Children in Glasgow and Edinburgh.

5.5 There have been several recent measles outbreaks in Northern Europe. In The Netherlands, there were 2961 notifications of measles in the period April 1999 to January 2000[55]. Serious complications were reported in 17% of cases, with 2.2% (68) requiring hospitalisation. There were three deaths. The most prevalent complications were pneumonia (193) and otitis media (196). The majority of cases (77%) occurred in the 1–9 year age group. The Republic of Ireland had an outbreak of measles in 2000, with over 1600 cases[56]. There were over 110 hospital admissions and three deaths.

5.6 Mumps can have serious complications, with neurological involvement in 10–20% of cases[57]. Before mmunisation, it was one of the main causes of acquired sensorineural deafness in childhood[58]. Inflammation of the testes in males is perhaps the most well-known complication, particularly when infected as an adult[59]. Approximately half of these cases may have some testicular atrophy, although reports of sterility are rare. Girls can get oophoritis (inflammation of the ovaries). Death is a rare outcome of mumps and is most often associated with mumps encephalitis. Again, there have been several recent mumps outbreaks in Europe: in Northern Ireland in 2001; in Switzerland in 1999; and in Spain and Portugal in 1998 and 1996 respectively.

5.7   Rubella is generally a mild illness, which, if acquired by mothers in early pregnancy, nevertheless can have devastating effects on unborn children[60]. The virus affects all fetal organs and can lead to serious birth defects. These include learning difficulties, cataracts, deafness, cardiac abnormalities, retardation of uterine growth and inflammatory lesions of the brain, liver, lungs and bone marrow. Maternal rubella infection in the first 10 weeks of pregnancy results in fetal damage in up to 90% of infants and multiple defects are common. Rare, non-pregnancy related, complications of rubella are encephalitis and idiopathic thrombocytopenic purpura (ITP). In 1993 an epidemic of rubella in Greece was followed approximately 6–7 months later by an outbreak of congenital rubella. Twenty-five cases were recorded (24.6 per 100,000 live births). All had serious symptoms, and seven died within 12 months[61].

The Current Immunisation Policy

5.8   The stated strategic objectives of the immunisation programme as a whole are: prevention of diseases at the individual level; control of disease at the population level; and elimination or eradication of the disease.

5.9   Eradication is a feasible long-term objective. For example, the World Health Organisation has adopted a resolution calling for global eradication of polio by the end of 2005. Three WHO Regions have not identified a single case caused by wild poliovirus for over 2 years. In the European Region the last case was in Turkey in November 1998. The UK, along with other countries of the European Region, is moving rapidly towards the certification of poliovirus eradication.

5.10 Once poliovirus transmission has been interrupted globally, the only potential source of wild poliovirus infection will be laboratories. Polio eradication will not be complete until all potential sources of poliovirus, including laboratory sources, are identified and contained.

5.11 Few medical procedures or treatments can compare with the enormous benefits to humanity from immunisation, one of the safest and most cost-effective of interventions[62]. However, no one claims that vaccines never have any side-effects. Vaccines can, very rarely, cause serious adverse effects. Such adverse effects are significantly more common following the natural disease. Immunisation programmes are in place all around the world precisely because, at both the individual and population levels, the benefits far outweigh any potential risk.

5.12 The Vaccine Damage Payments Act 1979 introduced a scheme of payments for those severely disabled as a result of vaccination. Where a person has been severely disabled as a result of vaccination, a tax-free one-off lump sum is payable (currently £100,000). This payment is not compensation, but is designed to ease the present and future burdens of those suffering from vaccine damage and their families. A payment under the scheme does not prejudice the right of the disabled person to pursue a claim for damages through the courts.

Prevention and control of measles, mumps and rubella

5.13 Prevention and control of measles, mumps and rubella are important elements of the routine childhood immunisation programme in most of the developed world. Annex 2 contains a snapshot of immunisation programmes in 17 European countries (the 15 EU Member States plus Norway and Switzerland), taken from the *Scientific and Technical Evaluation of Vaccination Programmes in the European Union* – known as the EUVAX Project Report. According to a questionnaire survey carried out by the EUVAC-NET in 2000, all countries in the EU have implemented a schedule of two doses of measles, mumps and rubella vaccine[63].

5.14 In Scotland, as elsewhere in the UK, two doses of the MMR vaccine are offered (at 12–15 months, and at 3–5 years), subject to the child having no medical contraindications and parental consent. This policy is based on independent medical and scientific advice to Health Ministers from the Joint Committee on Vaccination and Immunisation, and recognition that expert advice from around the world endorses MMR as the safest and most effective vaccine in order to protect all children from these very serious, and potentially fatal, diseases. There are of course some children who should not have MMR (see paragraphs 5.22 et seq). These children can only be protected by the fact that most others are vaccinated, and unlikely to be carrying these diseases.

5.15 The aim of vaccination in the individual is to produce long-lasting immunity so that, if a person is subsequently exposed to wild viruses, he or she is able to rapidly prevent the virus multiplying and thereby avoiding illness. If a mother has been vaccinated against measles, mumps or rubella or has experienced natural infection, her blood will contain antibodies designed to target and eliminate these specific viruses. During pregnancy, these antibodies enter the unborn child, but they usually decline between 6 and 12 months of age. If MMR vaccine is given when a baby's blood contains these antibodies, the vaccine will effectively be inactivated before the baby is able to mount its own long-lasting immune response. This is why the first dose of MMR is offered at 12–15 months. As such, children under 1 year old (and indeed unimmunised pregnant women) rely on population protection for their personal protection.

5.16 The rationale for administering a second MMR dose at 3–5 years is based on the fact that, on an individual level, MMR does not provide protection against measles in up to 10% of children who receive one dose. Furthermore, at present more than 10% of children do not receive that first dose of MMR. Both of these groups remain susceptible to measles after one dose of MMR vaccine has been offered. As such, on a community level, it is not possible to achieve population protection and effective disease control with a one-dose schedule. If approximately 90% of children receive MMR, and in 10% of these it fails to work, only 81% will be immune after one doses i.e. 19% unprotected. More than 90% of the population need to be immune for measles to be eliminated. If population protection is not achieved, breakthrough outbreaks will occur among non-recipients, non-responders, infants aged less than 1 year who are too young to be vaccinated and immunocompromised children in whom MMR is contraindicated. For these reasons, a two-dose schedule is recommended in the UK. A second MMR vaccination protects most children who do not respond to the first dose – around 90% will respond to the second dose. This reduces the chance of an individual remaining susceptible from 1 in 10 to 1 in 100 after a second dose. A further benefit is that it boosts the antibody levels of those children who did respond to the first dose. Finally, by offering a second dose of MMR vaccine, those children who did not receive a first dose get a second chance to be immunised. (The corresponding figure is approximately 10% for mumps and 5% for rubella, but the rationale is explained using the figures for measles only for the sake of simplicity). In summary, 99% of those vaccinated will be protected by two doses of MMR.

First dose of MMR protects at least 90% of eligible children against measles, at least 90% against mumps, and at least 95% against rubella.

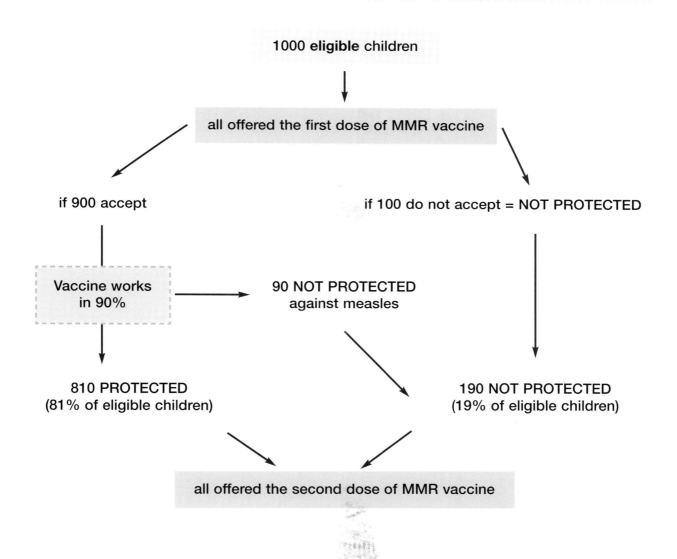

5.17 MMR immunisation uptake rates are calculated and published quarterly, for quarters ending March, June, September and December, and annually. The cohorts used in the calculation of the uptake rates are based on all children reaching a specified age who were registered on the systems at the end of the reporting period. As such, quarterly figures to the end of December 2001 showed MMR uptake at 86.6% across Scotland. These figures relate to children who have reached age 2 during the period in question, although these children may have been immunised any time up to 15 months previously. The latest annual figures[64] are:

Year	Primary immunisation	Pre-school booster
2001	89%	88.3%
2000	93%	90%

MMR – serious adverse effects

5.18 Few medical procedures or treatments can compare with the enormous benefits to humanity from immunisation. It is one of the safest and most cost-effective of interventions. Very rarely, MMR can cause serious adverse effects. Such adverse effects are significantly more common following the natural disease as the following table[6] shows.

Conditions	Children affected after the natural disease	Children affected after the first dose of MMR
Febrile convulsions (temperature fits)	1 in 200	1 in 1000
Meningitis/encephalitis	1 in 1000 (measles, mumps encephalitis) 1 in 20 (mumps meningitis) 1 in 6000 (rubella encephalitis)	less than 1 in 1,000,000
Conditions affecting blood clotting (ITP)	1 in 3000 (rubella) 1 in 6000 (measles)	1 in 22,000
Severe allergic response (anaphylaxis)	–	1 in 100,000
SSPE (a delayed complication of measles that causes brain damage and death)	1 in 8000 (children under 2)	0
Deaths	1 in 2500 to 1 in 5000 (measles; higher in children under 1) 1–2 in 1000 for measles in recent years	0

5.19 Idiopathic thrombocytopenic purpura (ITP) is a condition that affects blood clotting due to a shortage of platelets in the blood. This causes the blood to clot less easily and can result in a purple rash on the patient's body as mild bleeding beneath the skin can occur. ITP often follows viral infection and most cases do not follow vaccination. ITP occurs much less frequently after MMR vaccination than it does after natural infection.

5.20 There is no increased risk from a second dose of MMR vaccine, with the exception of allergic reactions. If complications were to occur, they would most likely be in the 5–10% of children who did not respond to the first dose: the weakened virus is killed as soon as it enters the body of a child who is already immune. The overall risk of complications after a second dose of MMR vaccine is therefore 90–95% less than that after the first dose.

5.21 As with any medical procedure, health care professionals are obliged to explain the advantages and disadvantages of vaccination[65]. The literature provided for parents and professionals describes all the known adverse effects of MMR. There are no other serious conditions for which there is evidence to indicate an increased risk after MMR immunisation. **The Expert Group considers that the information provided to parents when they are invited to bring their child to be immunised should now be reviewed and regularly updated.**

Children who should not have MMR

5.22 There are, of course, some children who should not have MMR (see box over), at all, or at a particular time.

5.23 As indicated above, in paragraph 5.3, measles can be a major cause of morbidity and mortality in children receiving immunosuppressive treatment, e.g. for leukaemia or after organ transplantation. In such circumstances, children are protected by the "population-immunity" that is a product of high immunisation uptake. Essentially, these children are protected by the fact that most other children are protected, and unlikely to be carrying the disease and infecting others.

5.24 In addition, as outlined in Chapter 4 (paragraph 4.26 *et seq*), existing legislation and policy allow a licensed importer to import a single measles or mumps vaccine and supply it in response to a doctor's prescription to meet the "special needs" of an individual patient, on the doctor's direct personal responsibility.

MMR CONTRAINDICATIONS (based on Immunisation Against Infectious Disease 1996 – The Green Book)

Absolute contraindications to MMR

– Children with untreated cancer or diseases of the immune system, those receiving immunosuppressive therapy or high dose steroids. This includes:

  • all patients currently being treated for malignant disease with chemotherapy or generalised radiotherapy or within 6 months of terminating such treatment;

  • all patients who have received an organ transplant and are currently on immunosuppressive treatment;

  • patients who within the previous 6 months have received a bone marrow transplant;

  • individuals on lower doses of steroids in combination with cytotoxic drugs – specialist advice should be sought;

  • individuals on lower doses of steroids or other immunosuppressants for prolonged periods or who because of underlying disease may be immunosuppressed and are at increased risk of infection. Specialist advice should be sought;

  • patients with evidence of impaired cell mediated immunity, e.g. HIV infection with current symptoms and various immunodeficiency syndromes;

– HIV positive individuals – specialist advice should be sought;

– Children with allergies to neomycin or kanamycin;

– Severe reaction to previous MMR.

(Like other live vaccines, MMR should not be administered to pregnant women.)

Reasons to postpone MMR

– Child is generally unwell with a fever;

– If a child is suffering from an acute illness, immunisation should be postponed until recovery has occurred;

– Child has had another live vaccine (including BCG) in the last 3 weeks;

– Child has been given an injection of immunoglobin in the last 3 months.

Not contraindications

– Egg allergy. Although tissue derived from eggs is used to grow the vaccine virus, as much as possible is removed. A number of scientific papers have been published which demonstrate the safety of MMR vaccine, even in children with a known severe egg allergy. MMR vaccine can be administered in hospital to children with a history of anaphylaxis to eggs, if there is particular parental concern;

– Previous history of measles;

– Minor infections without fever or systemic upset.

5.25 The Expert Group recognises that some health professionals and some parents of children with IBD and/or ASD have particular concerns about immunising children with IBD and/or ASD and their siblings. **The Group recommends that CSM and JCVI should, taking account of ongoing and future research into the causes of IBD and ASD, continue to keep these vaccination contraindications under review.**

A Framework of Principles for Immunisation Policy

5.26 The Group accepted and endorsed, without reservation the high-level strategic objectives of immunisation:

- prevention of disease at the individual level;
- control of disease at the population level; <u>and</u>
- elimination or eradication of disease.

But it considered that a broader range of explicit principles should underpin immunisation policy, albeit that some will have greater priority than others at any given point in time.

5.27 In the course of discussing these issues, the Expert Group developed the following framework of principles for the public/childhood immunisation programme in order to guide its thinking:

A. A rigorous evidence-based and transparent process should validate the safety, quality and efficacy of vaccines that are offered within the programme, in order to provide treatment and care which represent best scientific and clinical practice. Scientific data about the safety, efficacy, and the nature and frequency of potential side-effects of vaccines should be in the public domain;

B. Citizens should have public interest representation on related scientific and medical advisory bodies;

C. Any vaccine used routinely in the programme should be licensed for use in the UK;

D. Any vaccine used in the programme should be subject to regular review;

E. Any adverse reactions should be systematically reported and monitored;

F. Any vaccine offered as part of the programme should be easily accessible and available to all, and free of charge to the patient; as such, equity of access is essential;

G. Vaccines should be administered on a voluntary basis, and only with the informed consent of the patient or, in the case of childhood immunisation, the parent or guardian of that child;

H. There should be general public support for the broad principle of the immunisation programme as a vital part of a public health strategy to prevent, control, eliminate or eradicate diseases at the population level;

I. Parents should be able to access personal advice when making a decision about vaccinating their child, should they wish;

J. The greatest number of children possible should be vaccinated to ensure population immunity and protect the population as a whole, and in particular the very few, very vulnerable children who cannot take a particular vaccine on health or philosophical grounds, and other vulnerable members of the population;

K. Any individual damaged by vaccines in the programme should be compensated on a no-fault basis.

5.28 The Expert Group found this sort of structure both challenging to define, and helpful. Given that the public debate about MMR will likely continue for some time, notwithstanding the substance of the scientific evidence, the Group considers that ongoing dialogue could usefully be structured and facilitated by an agreed, transparent framework along these lines.

5.29 As such, **the Expert Group recommends that the JCVI should:**

- **develop core principles for immunisation policy in order to provide all interested parties with a clear framework against which any future policy options might be assessed in an open and transparent manner; and**

- **continue to publish the conclusions of its regular review of the scientific evidence relating to the safety and efficacy of MMR, and seek to improve on existing arrangements for publicising that material.**

5.30 The Expert Group also recommends that Health Ministers (in the UK Government and devolved administrations) should urgently implement existing plans to extend arrangements for appointing members, to the Joint Committee on Vaccination and Immunisation, who are non-medical experts and/or members of the general public.

5.31 The Expert Group also looks to The Scottish Executive to ensure that the level and quality of information available to parents in Scotland whose children are due to be immunised against measles, mumps and rubella, are significantly and urgently improved by:

- **ensuring that all parents receive basic factual information about MMR (for example, contraindications, the risks posed by measles, mumps and rubella, and the risks of adverse reactions) with the invitation to bring their child for immunisation;**

- **ensuring that all parents know that they can, and should, discuss any related questions with their GP or health visitor in order to make an informed choice about immunisation;**

- asking HEBS to evaluate and develop *"the MMR discussion pack"*, in order to maintain and enhance the currency and accuracy of the information, training and support provided to GPs and other health professionals, in relation to the medical science underpinning the immunisation programme;

- requiring NHS Boards to put in place systematic arrangements for providing further advice to parents who, despite discussions with their GP or other health professional, have concerns and questions about MMR or the particular circumstances of their child.

Alternative Immunisation Policies and their Consequences

5.32 There are, in essence, five immunisation policies which might be considered as an alternative to the current policy: no immunisation; compulsory immunisation; deferral of MMR; a choice between either MMR or single vaccines; or single vaccines. The considerations associated with each of these options are set out in the table below and in more detail in the text that follows.

No immunisation

5.33 A small proportion of people have philosophical objections to immunisation. Others, as indicated above, cannot be immunised on medical grounds. None of the submissions presented to the Expert Group question the merit of immunisation against measles, mumps and rubella, more generally. There is therefore a clear and overwhelming consensus that immunisation has been one of the major public health successes of the last century, and that the "no immunisation" policy is not tenable at a population level, because that would:

- run counter to scientific and medical best practice, and what we know of the views of the population as a whole;

- lead to a decrease in population immunity and guarantee an increase in the incidence of measles, mumps and rubella.

Compulsory vaccination

5.34 A small proportion of people have philosophical objections to immunisation. Others, as indicated above, cannot be immunised on medical grounds. As such, there would have to be some exceptions to this policy. None of the submissions presented to the Expert Group supported compulsion.

5.35 The Expert Group concluded that such a policy is not consistent with key elements of the framework of principles for immunisation policy. On a practical level, it is not self-evident that it would lead to higher levels of immunisation. More substantively, it runs counter to the Expert Group's core principle that vaccines should be administered on a voluntary basis.

Options, assessed against principles from the immunisation framework

Options, assessed against principles from the immunisation framework						
Principle	**No immunisation**	**Compulsory vaccination**	**Deferral of MMR**	**MMR or single vaccines**	**Single vaccines**	**Current policy**
A - evidence-based validation of safety, quality and efficacy	No	Yes	Yes	Unlicensed vaccines have not been assessed by the MCA against the criteria of safety, quality and efficacy.		Yes
B - public representation scientific advisory bodies	Planned					
C - Licensed for use in the UK	Not relevant	Yes		Unlicensed vaccines have not been assessed by the MCA against the criteria of safety, quality and efficacy. Manufacture and supply issues would need to be addressed for licensed single vaccines		Yes
D – vaccine subject to regular review				Yes For MMR		
E - adverse reactions monitored		Yes				
F - Accessible and available, free of charge		Yes		Manufacture and supply issues would need to be addressed for licensed single vaccines		Yes
G - Voluntary		No		Yes		
H - General public support		No		Not Known		Yes But open to interpretation
I - Access to advice	Not relevant	Yes				
J - ensure population immunity	No	No Compulsion does not guarantee high uptake	No	Not Known		Yes Albeit below optimum 95% uptake
K – Compensation available.	Not relevant	Yes		Yes If licensed and included in compensation scheme		Yes

Deferral of MMR

5.36 There are, as indicated at paragraph 5.22 et seq above, clinical reasons for postponing MMR. However, the rationale for deferral set out in submissions presented to the Expert Group relate to two separate arguments.

5.37 The first argument is that there is merit in deferring MMR until a child's immune system is "better developed". However, the scientific evidence currently available does not support the conclusion that component vaccines either interfere adversely with each other, or weaken or overwhelm an infant's immune system.While concern has been raised that three live viral vaccines administered together may overwhelm the immune system, the available data that exists does not support this hypothesis. Studies have been conducted where vaccines have been given either separately or at the same time as MMR which directly addresses this issue. If MMR overwhelmed the immune system one would expect reduced responses to vaccines administered at the same time. This is not the case[66].

5.38 The second argument is that deferral allows evidence of standard development (or otherwise) to become more apparent. This is the "coincidence factor" referred to by the HCCC. The major difficulty associated with this strategy, notwithstanding the scientific evidence of no link between MMR and autism, is that, on average, autism is diagnosed at around 4 years of age in the UK. Deferral beyond that age would leave children unprotected for an extended period of time, and put such children, and others, at greater risk of infection.

5.39 The Expert Group recognises that deferring MMR immunisation could be considered both by The Executive (for Scotland as a whole) and by individual parents (for their child). However, the Expert Group concluded that such a policy is not in accord with key elements of the framework of principles for immunisation policy. It is not supported by current scientific evidence, and it leaves children unprotected and at greater risk of infection for longer than is necessary.

MMR or single vaccines

5.40 The Expert Group recognises that some parents wish to be given the choice of a single vaccine for their children, because:

- of concerns about autism; or
- of concerns about the concurrent administration of three live vaccines; or
- both methods are considered to be equally efficacious and effective; or
- it is a pragmatic way to acknowledge some or all of those concerns and at the same time increase vaccine uptake and population immunity; or
- choice is a civil right.

5.41 Before addressing these considerations in turn, it is important to recognise a very practical consideration, which is that although single antigen measles and mumps vaccines were previously available in the UK, they are not currently manufactured to UK licence specifications. As such, before this alternative policy could be introduced, vaccine manufacturers would have to begin to produce these vaccines in sufficient quantity and to that standard of quality control. It is not clear how long that would take.

5.42 A case for making single vaccines available by popular choice, as opposed to the clinical judgement of a health professional (as at present, see paragraph 5.24), cannot be sustained on the basis of the available scientific evidence. As indicated in earlier chapters, there is no proven scientific link between the measles, mumps and rubella (MMR) vaccine and autism or Crohn's disease. Another important factor is that even if there were substantive scientific evidence to support the original hypothesised link between autism and measles virus, there is no evidence that the single vaccine option would actually be any safer. Similarly, the scientific evidence supports the conclusion that the component viruses do not interfere with each other[66].

5.43 The efficacy of MMR would be the same as the constituent single vaccines, in relation to providing protection for an individual, subject to issues of manufacture and quality control (which is, as indicated in Chapter 4, a key feature of UK licensing arrangements, but not the importation of unlicensed medicines. A number of different strains are manufactured, and it is important to compare like with like).

5.44 The comparative effectiveness of single vaccines, as part of a childhood immunisation programme is more open to question. There are a number of generally acknowledged drawbacks relating to the issues of both increased susceptibility whilst awaiting immunisation, and the likelihood of vaccinations being missed altogether as six vaccinations would be required, rather than two (and some might not appreciate the importance of giving mumps vaccine to girls, or the rubella vaccine to boys). This would decrease the level of population protection. This is particularly true, if an interval of 1 year was left between vaccinations, as has been recommended by Mr Wakefield and others. The concurrent administration of separate vaccines for measles, mumps and rubella has never been formally tested for either efficacy or safety. Therefore, the best time interval to leave between doses, and the risk of vaccine associated adverse events, are simply not known. In addition, six vaccines would inevitably lead to increased risk of local reactions at the injection site; and increased trauma to the child.

5.45 Advocates of single vaccines maintain that their availability would increase the overall level of population immunity, as they believe that almost all those recently refusing MMR immunisation would consent to separate vaccinations. On the other hand, most health professionals believe that making single vaccines available in this way may well undermine public confidence in immunisation against measles, mumps and rubella, in general. The current level of MMR uptake can be used as an argument either way: it may signal significant public concern about MMR; or nearly 90% of parents may be demonstrating their support for MMR. What is clear is that if single vaccines were available by popular choice, as opposed to the clinical judgement of a health professional (as at present, see paragraph 5.24), protection at individual and population level would depend on the relative proportions of the target population embarking on the MMR and single vaccine programmes.

5.46 Essentially, the extent to which population immunity would be affected by allowing such a choice would depend on several factors:

i) the extent to which this would result in increased vaccine uptake by those who refuse to accept reassurances over the safety of MMR and currently thus leave their children, and others, unprotected;

ii) the extent to which this would change the vaccine uptake decisions taken by those who currently accept MMR;

iii) the extent to which multiple visits would result in increased default; and

iv) the extent to which leaving a space between vaccines rather than using concurrent administration would open up a window within which temporarily unvaccinated children would be at significantly elevated vulnerability to infection.

5.47 The Expert Group noted that the Scottish Centre for Infection and Environmental Health (SCIEH), in collaboration with the University of Strathclyde, is undertaking research with the aim of developing mathematical models which might help demonstrate the range of possible outcomes, for the population as a whole, arising out of decisions made by individual parents. This work is at a very early stage, but in time may help us all to achieve a better understanding of these public health policy options and their effect on the level of immunity in the population. **The Expert Group looks to The Scottish Executive to ensure that appropriate resources are provided to allow this work to be carried forward.**

5.48 The civil rights argument is not, *on its own*, compelling, when considered in the light of the Expert Group's framework of principles. It is consistent with some, but not all. The Expert Group recognised that it falls to the Scottish Executive to struggle with the question: given finite resources should the state meet the cost of an individual's desire to access vaccines which could be less effective within the context of an immunisation programme, and which may carry higher risks to the individual and society? Nevertheless, representatives of children with autism and their carers on the Expert Group, including SSA and NAS, were clear that, despite there being no proven scientific evidence of a link between MMR and ASD, on the basis of the currently available evidence, parental concerns are now such as to warrant JCVI revisiting the question whether there should be alternative immunisation arrangements for such families.

5.49 The Expert Group recognised the risks of introducing a dual arrangement for immunisation, for the reasons set out above (paragraphs 5.45–6). The Expert Group also recognises that the Scottish Executive has a duty of care to take account of the body of scientific and medical evidence in order to provide treatment and care which represents best clinical practice. As such, the Expert Group concluded that this alternative immunisation policy is not consistent with key elements of its framework of principles.

Single vaccines instead of MMR

5.50 None of the submissions presented to the Expert Group supported the option of single vaccines replacing MMR in the childhood vaccination programme. However, it is a valid option.

5.51 Most of the considerations outlined above would obviously apply:

- before this alternative policy could be introduced vaccine manufacturers would have to begin to produce these vaccines in sufficient quantity; it is not clear how long that would take; and

- a compelling case for single vaccines cannot be sustained on the basis of the available scientific evidence, efficacy or effectiveness.

5.52 As such, the Expert Group concluded that this alternative immunisation policy is not consistent with key elements of its framework of principles.

Chapter 5 – Summary of Key Points

The success of immunisation against measles, mumps and rubella has led to a decline in the incidence of these diseases. As such, the serious associated risks may not be fully appreciated.

There are, of course some children who should not have MMR, at all, or at a particular time. Children receiving immunosuppressive treatment, e.g. for leukaemia or after organ transplantation, are protected by the "population-immunity" that is a product of high immunisation uptake. Children under 1 year old, and unimmunised pregnant women, also rely on population protection for their personal protection.

In considering the range and implications of alternative immunisation policies, the Expert Group developed a framework of principles to guide its thinking. A published JCVI framework of principles may inform and structure further public debate about MMR.

Although single antigen measles and mumps vaccine were previously available in the UK, they are not currently manufactured to UK licence specifications.

The Expert Group considered five alternative immunisation policies:

- a "no immunisation" policy is not tenable;

- no one advocated compulsory vaccination or single vaccines replacing MMR;

- deferring MMR immunisation is not best practice supported by current scientific evidence, and leaves children unprotected and at greater risk of infection for longer;

- the case for making single vaccines available by popular choice (the MMR or single vaccines option), as opposed to the clinical judgement of a health professional (as at present), cannot be sustained on the available scientific evidence. The efficacy of MMR would be the same as the constituent single vaccines, in relation to providing protection for an individual, subject to issues of manufacture and quality control. The comparative effectiveness of single vaccines is more open to question. It is clear that, if single vaccines were made available in this way protection at individual and population level would depend on:

  i)   the extent to which this would result in increased vaccine uptake by those who have concerns about MMR and currently leave their children unprotected;

  ii) the extent to which this would change the vaccine uptake decisions taken by those who currently accept MMR;

  iii) the extent to which multiple visits would result in increased default; and

  iv) the extent to which leaving a space between vaccines rather than using concurrent administration would open up a window within which temporarily unvaccinated children would be at significantly elevated vulnerability to infection.

The Expert Group has recommended a range of measures to both continue to review research evidence as it develops, and to give parents better and timely information.

6 Questions, Answers and Next Steps

This chapter:

- answers the specific questions posed by HCCC (paragraph 6.1 to 6.2); and
- lists all the recommendations made by the Expert Group (paragraph 6.3 to 6.4).

Questions and Answers

6.1   The "matters raised by the Health and Community Care Committee" are largely defined by a series of questions posed by the Committee, which broadly underpin the formal remit of the Expert Group. In considering how best to provide "answers", the Expert Group recognised both the underlying complexity of the questions (and therefore any response) and the value of brief, factual statements in plain language.

6.2   The Expert Group considers it important to stress that the relatively brief answers set out in the following pages build on the more detailed information and comment set out in earlier chapters. Appropriate cross-references to relevant sections are therefore provided.

1.1   What is the scientific basis for the recommended time period between vaccines?

The HCCC report noted that there was a divergence of opinion (among those who presented evidence) on the recommended time period between the proposed administration of separate vaccines for measles, mumps and rubella, ranging from 6 weeks to 12 months.

JCVI recommends simultaneous administration or an interval of 3 weeks between live vaccines. However, the Expert Group found no scientific evidence to support any specific time period between the administration of separate vaccines for measles, mumps and rubella. Therefore, the best time interval to leave between doses, and the related risk of vaccine associated adverse events, are simply not known.

See also paragraphs 5.13 *et seq*, and 5.40 *et seq*.

1.2   Would a choice of single vaccines increase or decrease the full uptake of the MMR vaccines, and what would the effect be on population immunity?

The Expert Group's framework of immunisation principles includes a commitment to vaccinating the greatest number of children possible, to ensure population immunity and protect the population as a whole, and in particular the very few, very vulnerable children who cannot take a particular vaccine on health or philosophical grounds.

The extent to which population immunity would be affected by making single vaccines available as an option within the childhood immunisation programme, would depend in our view on four factors:

i)   the extent to which this would result in increased vaccine uptake by those who do not currently accept reassurances over the safety of MMR and currently thus leave their children unprotected;

ii)   the extent to which this would result in decreased MMR vaccine uptake by those who currently accept the safety of MMR, thus leaving their children temporarily unvaccinated and unprotected against two of these three diseases;

iii)   the extent to which leaving a space between vaccines, rather than using concurrent administration, would open up a window within which temporarily unvaccinated children would be at significantly elevated vulnerability to infection; and

iv)   the extent to which multiple visits would result in increased default from some or all of the vaccines being administered.

In the 1970s there were concerns – later shown to be unfounded – about the safety of pertussis (whooping cough) vaccine. Parents then were offered a choice of vaccines, with or without the pertussis component. Uptake of whooping cough vaccine fell to 48% in Scotland and the control of pertussis took 15 years to recover. It is estimated that there were 100,000 cases of whooping cough in Scotland during this period, thousands were admitted to hospital, and there were up to 75 deaths.

As such, based on current MMR uptake levels, it is reasonable to conclude that population immunity would suffer as a result of a decision to make single vaccines more widely available on demand. Such a fall in population immunity inevitably increases the risk of an outbreak.

See also paragraphs 5.13 *et seq* and 5.40–49.

1.3 Is it administrative convenience or best clinical practice to administer three vaccines in one visit?

The HCCC report stated that the French system suggests the possibility of giving the measles vaccine singly (from 9 months onwards), followed by the mumps and rubella vaccines, or indeed by the combined MMR vaccine at a later stage. **That is not wholly correct.** The policy, which we understand may be under review, is described below.

First, however, it is important to note that the aim of vaccination in the individual is to produce long-lasting immunity so that if a person is subsequently exposed to wild viruses he or she is able rapidly to prevent the virus multiplying and thereby avoiding illness. If a mother has been vaccinated against measles, mumps or rubella, or has experienced natural infection, her blood will contain antibodies designed to target and eliminate these specific viruses. During pregnancy, these antibodies enter the unborn child, but they usually decline between 6 and 12 months of age. If MMR vaccine is given when a baby's blood contains these antibodies, the vaccine will effectively be inactivated before the baby is able to mount its own long-lasting immune response.

The French policy is to offer MMR at 12–15 months and a second dose at 3-6 years. In addition, single measles vaccine is offered at 9 months to children in crèches because they may be at greater risk. This is designed to protect those children whose maternal protection has worn off, but it is recognised that some children will not get long-lasting immunity. This is why all French children are offered MMR at 12-15 months and again at 3–6 years.

Taking account of the answer at 1.2 above, it is both administrative convenience and best clinical practice to administer MMR (three vaccines in one visit) because it:

- provides protection against all three diseases, and avoids a window within which temporarily unvaccinated children would be at significantly elevated vulnerability to infection; and reduces the risk of missing a dose completely;

- minimises the trauma to the child;

- minimises the risk of local reactions at the injection site.

Expert medical advice, both here and internationally, confirms that MMR remains the safest and most effective way to protect children from these very serious and potentially fatal diseases.

See also paragraphs 5.13 *et seq* and 5.40 *et seq*.

2.1   Is there any benefit in deferring the MMR vaccine until the immunity system is better developed?

2.2   If so, and taking into account the presence of the "coincidence factor", what is the optimal time for administration of the combined vaccine?

The HCCC report highlighted a "coincidence factor" arising because the first parental concerns in children subsequently diagnosed with ASD are generally recognised at 14–20 months, and this coincides with the administration of the MMR vaccine.

There are some children who should not have MMR, for example, because they have untreated cancer or diseases of the immune system, are receiving immunosuppressive therapy or high dose steroids, have allergies to specific antibiotics (such as neomycin or kanamycin) or have reacted severely to a previous MMR.

There are also clinical reasons for postponing MMR, such as if the child is unwell with a fever, has been given an injection of immunoglobulin in the last 3 months, or had another live vaccine (including BCG) in the last 3 weeks.

There is, however, no substantive case for deferring immunisation until the immunity system is "better developed". The scientific evidence currently available confirms that component viruses do not either interfere adversely with each other, nor weaken nor overwhelm an infant's immune system, and the immune system is reliably able to cope with the multiple vaccines. The scientific evidence currently available does not support a link between MMR and autism.

Similarly, there is no compelling case for deferring immunisation to allow evidence of standard development (or otherwise) to become more apparent. Notwithstanding the scientific evidence of no link between MMR and autism, on average ASD is diagnosed at around 4 years of age in the UK. Deferral beyond that age would leave children unprotected for an extended period of time, and put such children, and others, at greater risk of infection.

The Expert Group recognises that deferring MMR immunisation is now a choice that some parents are making of their own accord. That decision leaves their child, other children (including those too young for immunisation) and other vulnerable members of the wider community, at greater risk of infection (taking account of the answer at 1.2–3 above and the more detailed account at paragraph 5.36 *et seq*).

See also paragraph 5.13 *et seq*.

3.1 Which countries allow single vaccinations?

3.2 What are the different uptake rates of the MMR vaccine across Europe and how have these affected population immunity and the threat of an epidemic?

The World Health Organization recommends MMR and does not recommend single vaccines where MMR is available. Single vaccines are in use in a number of countries, particularly those in the developing world where economic, social and other factors combine to produce a different assessment of the interaction between risk, benefit and cost. Put simply, some countries cannot afford MMR. In most of the developing world, monovalent or bivalent MR vaccines are more typically used.

Prevention and control of measles, mumps and rubella are an important element of the routine childhood immunisation programme in most of the developed world. Annex 2 contains details of immunisation programmes in 17 European countries (the 15 EU Member States plus Norway and Switzerland), taken from the Scientific and Technical Evaluation of Vaccination Programmes in the European Union – known as the EUVAX Project Report. As indicated above (in response to 1.3) in France children are given a single measles vaccine at around 9 months old if they are in a nursery. Those children are then offered two further MMR vaccinations.

In Japan, from 1992 to 1997, there were 79 measles deaths[67]. MMR vaccine was introduced in Japan in 1989, but withdrawn in 1993, as it contained the Urabe strain of mumps. Japan currently recommends single measles and single rubella vaccines to be given at the same time, as, unlike in the UK, no suitable alternative MMR vaccine is available. Uptake of measles vaccine in Japan was 75% in 1996, increasing to 81% in the year 2000. These low vaccine uptake rates have led to small-scale epidemics consistently occurring in some regions. For example, in Okinawa, 675 children were hospitalised with measles during the period September 1998 to October 1999. 98% of these children had not been immunised, and there were eight deaths. In Japan overall, there has been an increase in the number of measles cases since 1993. In the year 2000, there were 22,497 notifications for measles, compared to 3,259 in 1990 and 13,219 in 1980. There was also a year on year increase in the number of deaths from measles in Japan in the years 1995 to 1999, following a pattern of general decline.

See also paragraph 5.13 *et seq.*

3.3 What is the effect on the community/public health if MMR vaccine rates fall?

If the rate of vaccination against measles, mumps and rubella falls, the effect on community/public health will be the return of these diseases in significant numbers with major consequences in terms of morbidity and mortality.

There have been several recent measles outbreaks in Northern Europe that illustrate the serious adverse implications of low uptake of MMR vaccine. With low vaccine uptake, the number of unvaccinated susceptible children builds up until the epidemic threshold is reached which, in the presence of measles or mumps or rubella virus, will allow for an outbreak.

In The Netherlands, there were 2961 notifications of measles in the period April 1999 to January 2000[68]. Cases occurred throughout the country, but were concentrated in areas where many parents object to vaccination on religious grounds. Almost all of the cases (95%) had not been vaccinated. Serious complications were reported for 17% of cases, with 2.2% (68) requiring hospitalisation. There were three deaths. The most prevalent complications were pneumonia (193) and otitis media (196). The majority of cases (77%) occurred in the 1–9-year age group, with an average age of 6 years. There have been previous measles epidemics in The Netherlands involving these religious communities in 1987/8 and 1992/93. Nationally, the figure for uptake of one dose of MMR vaccine is 96%. However, this outbreak illustrates that even with good overall population uptake; if there are "micropopulations" of unvaccinated children, of sufficient number to allow virus transmission, outbreaks will still occur.

The Republic of Ireland had an outbreak of measles in 2000, with over 1,600 cases[69]. Action taken to curb transmission included a vaccination awareness campaign, which was actually planned before the start of the outbreak, and a lowering of the age for MMR vaccine administration from the routine of 15 months to 6 months in the North Dublin area, and to 12 months in the South Dublin, Kildare and Wicklow areas. The figure for uptake of MMR vaccine in the Eastern Health Board, the area with most cases, was 74.4%. There were over 110 hospital admissions and three deaths.

There have been several recent mumps outbreaks in Europe: in Northern Ireland in 2001; in Switzerland in 1999; and in Spain and Portugal in 1998 and 1996 respectively.

In 1993 an epidemic of rubella in Greece was followed approximately 6–7 months later by an outbreak of congenital rubella. Twenty-five cases were recorded (24.6 per 100,000 live births). All had serious symptoms, and seven died within 12 months[61]. In Greece, there had been a "mixed" immunisation schedule for MMR, whereby the private sector provided MMR and the public sector provided single measles vaccine and rubella for teenage girls. The epidemic of rubella and the related outbreak of congenital rubella have been attributed to shortcomings in the public immunisation programme.

There have, of course, been measles outbreaks in the UK early in 2002: 95 cases in England, the majority (73) occurring in London; and three in Scotland – the first such cases for 2 years. See also paragraph 5.2 *et seq.*

3.4   Have there been any studies done in France on those children who receive measles vaccine only (at 9–12 months) followed by the MMR vaccine in relation to evidence of an increase in the incidence of autism?

No – few studies of population prevalence of autism have been carried out in France, and those that were done did not consider MMR.

4.1   If not caused by the MMR vaccine, then why the steep rises in autism?

4.2   Is the rise in autism as a result of better diagnosis?

4.3   Does it reflect the adoption of a much broader concept of autism?

4.4   Is it the case that autism is now identified at a much earlier age?

4.5   Why is autism rising, while the vaccine rates remain constant?

The HCCC report acknowledged that there is little dispute that there has been a rise in diagnoses of autism, but there is uncertainty about why there has been this rise.

As indicated, more substantively, in both the MRC Review of Autism Research and the PHIS Needs Assessment, in part this uncertainty exists because diagnosis is based on behavioural criteria and there is no biological confirmatory test for ASD (although in some cases genetic testing can be helpful). The MRC Review of Autism confirms that the likely causes of apparent increases in prevalence are:

- changes in diagnostic practice; and
- changes in public and professional awareness; and
- methodological differences between studies.

Whether these factors are sufficient to account for increased numbers of identified individuals, or whether there has been a rise in actual numbers affected, is as yet unclear. See also paragraph 2.8 *et seq*.

4.6 Are health checks and Health Visitor Records as presently held and updated, adequate to pick up signs of autism?

Diagnosis is based on behavioural criteria, and there is no biological confirmatory test for ASD (although in some cases genetic testing can be helpful).

The focus of routine developmental screening is primarily on motor, sensory and other physical aspects of development and is not sufficiently detailed with respect to early social aspects of development to identify reliably early concerns. This role normally falls to Health Visitors, and as many are good observers of social functioning, such difficulties are often detected where they are present. Parental concern is a most useful indicator of such early difficulties.

It is clear that early screening methods are not wholly effective in detecting the early signs of autism. The Expert Group welcomes the (UK) National Initiative on Autism: Screening and Assessment (NIASA), which has been set up by the Royal College of Paediatrics and Child Health and the Faculty of Child and Adolescent Psychiatry, Royal College of Psychiatrists, with the support of the National Autistic Society (NAS) and the All-Party Parliamentary Group on Autism (APPGA).

The Expert Group has endorsed the detailed recommendations set out in the PHIS Autistic Spectrum Disorders Needs Assessment Report, and in particular those relating to improved diagnosis and management of ASD, and the need for a more coherent and systematic approach to training health, education and social care professionals, better and in more appropriate numbers. See also paragraph 2.43 *et seq*.

5.1 *Would the single vaccines, given at intervals, lead to delayed and incomplete courses leading to outbreaks of disease resulting in disease and disability?*

The HCCC report acknowledged that, where single vaccines are used, exposure to infection persists in the intervals between each immunisation and single vaccines may be less effective than the combined vaccine. This applies, in particular, to certain types of mumps vaccines where the strain used produces a very poor antibody response.

The Expert Group agrees that with any immunisation policy involving single vaccines there would be a (relative) increase in susceptibility whilst awaiting immunisation and also in the likelihood of vaccinations being missed altogether as six vaccinations would be required, rather than two. Six vaccines would inevitably lead to increased risk of local reactions at the injection site and increased trauma to the child.

However, as indicated above in the answer to 2.1, there is no definitive answer to this question, as the outcome is variable and would depend critically on levels of vaccine uptake and the pattern of population demographics.

The 1970s experience with the pertussis (whooping cough) vaccine may be illustrative of what might happen. At that time there were concerns – later shown to be unfounded – about the safety of pertussis (whooping cough) vaccine. Parents then were offered a choice of vaccines, with or without the pertussis component. Uptake of whooping cough vaccine fell to 48% in Scotland, and the control of pertussis took 15 years to recover. It is estimated that there were 100,000 cases of whooping cough in Scotland during this period, thousands were admitted to hospital, and there were up to 75 deaths.

See also paragraph 5.40 *et seq*.

5.2 Are single vaccines any less effective than the triple vaccine?

The efficacy of the three individual vaccines in MMR is similar to that of the **licensed** single measles and mumps vaccines, which are not marketed in the UK and the **licensed** rubella vaccine, which is.

The imported **unlicensed** single measles and mumps vaccines currently being administered have not been assessed by the MCA for safety, quality and efficacy.

In theory, the efficacy of MMR would be the same as the constituent single vaccines, in relation to providing protection for an individual, subject to issues of manufacture and quality control (which is, as indicated in Chapter 4, a key feature of UK licensing arrangements, but not the importation of unlicensed medicines. A number of different strains are manufactured, and it is important to take care to compare like with like).

However, all the evidence suggests that single vaccines are less **effective** than MMR in providing individual and population immunity against all three diseases. There are a number of generally acknowledged drawbacks associated with single vaccines, relating to the issues of both increased susceptibility whilst awaiting immunisation, and the likelihood of vaccinations being missed altogether as six vaccinations would be required, rather than two (and some might not appreciate the importance of giving mumps vaccine to girls, or the rubella vaccine to boys). This would decrease the level of population protection.

The concurrent administration of separate vaccines for measles, mumps and rubella has never been formally tested for either efficacy or safety. Therefore, the best time interval to leave between doses, and the risk of vaccine associated adverse events, are simply not known. In addition, six vaccines would inevitably lead to increased risk of local reactions at the injection site; and increased trauma to the child.

The Expert Group concluded that this alternative immunisation policy is not wholly consistent with key elements of its framework of principles for immunisation policy.

See also paragraphs 4.30 *et seq*, 5.26 *et seq*, and 5.43.

6.1 Should single vaccines be made available to patients on a named basis?

6.2 If so, what additional criteria should be used (family history of autism, known allergies, low immunity, existing bowel problems)?

The HCCC report highlighted the importance of advice on whether certain individuals are at risk. It suggested, for example, that because these (both MMR and single) vaccines are cultured using an egg base, it is contraindicated for those with an egg allergy.

In fact, as indicated by default in the response to 2.1–2 above, egg allergy is not a contraindication. There are some children who should not have MMR, or indeed single vaccines, namely those who have untreated cancer or diseases of the immune system, are receiving immunosuppressive therapy or high dose steroids, have allergies to specific antibiotics (for example, neomycin or kanamycin) or reacted severely to a previous MMR. See paragraph 5.22 *et seq*. Any decision to extend these contraindications would depend upon advice from the JCVI, CSM and MCA.

Existing legislation allows a licensed importer to import an unlicensed monocomponent vaccine and supply it in response to a doctor's prescription to meet the "special needs" of an individual patient, on the doctor's direct personal responsibility. See paragraphs 4.26 *et seq* and 5.24.

The Expert Group recognises that some health professionals and some parents of children with IBD and/or autism have particular concerns about immunising children with IBD and/or autism and siblings. The current evidence base does not provide any substantive case for extending existing contraindications. That said, the Expert Group has recommended that JCVI and CSM should, taking account of ongoing and future research into the causes of IBD and autism, continue to keep these vaccination contraindications under review.

6.3 Could the increased use of antibiotics in children affect the immune system and therefore the response to MMR?

There is no scientific evidence currently available to indicate that component viruses either interfere adversely with each other, or weaken or overwhelm an infant's immune system. See also paragraphs 5.13 and 5.37 *et seq*.

Similarly, the scientific evidence currently available does not support the conclusion that children taking antibiotics should not be vaccinated. The origin of this concern seems to be the recommendation that immunisation should be deferred in an acutely unwell child[70]. Many acutely ill children are given antibiotics, and the taking of antibiotics has become a proxy for a substantial illness. However, it is now a common belief that antibiotics somehow interfere with immunisation. There is no logical reason why a child taking antibiotics cannot be immunised, provided he or she is well on the day of immunisation. Interestingly, even the standard advice is often misunderstood, with people inferring that acute illness interferes with immunisation. The little evidence that exists is ambivalent. The true reason for deferral is to avoid difficulties in diagnosis and management, should a child's condition worsen after immunisation.

6.4 What would be the effect on population immunity of excluding these groups from MMR vaccination programmes?

This question relates back to the examples of possible additional contraindication criteria in the HCCC report (namely, family history of autism, known allergies, low immunity, existing bowel problems).

Any decision to extend current contraindications would depend upon the advice to Scottish Ministers of the Joint Committee on Vaccination and Immunisation, the Committee on Safety of Medicines and/or the Medicines Control Agency. The Expert Group considers that current medical and scientific knowledge would not support or enable existing contraindications to be extended. That said, the Expert Group has recommended that JCVI and CSM should, taking account of ongoing and future research into the causes of IBD and autism, continue to keep these vaccination contraindications under review.

Any decision to increase the relative proportion of children who cannot be vaccinated against measles, mumps and rubella would have some effect on population immunity. The nature of such change cannot be predicted precisely, because it depends on a complex interaction of a number of factors including the proportion of children to be so excluded, and the vaccine uptake rate amongst those eligible to be vaccinated.

It is a truism that the risk of an outbreak increases as the number of unvaccinated, susceptible children builds up.

See also paragraphs 5.13 *et seq* and 5.22 *et seq*.

6.5   What are the arguments for and against adopting the system exemplified in those attending state nursery schools in France?

As indicated above (in response to 1.3) the French policy (which may be under review) is to offer MMR at 12–15 months and a second dose at 3–6 years. In addition single measles vaccine is offered at 9 months to children in crèches, because they may be at greater risk. This is designed to protect those children whose maternal protection has worn off, but it is recognised that some children will not get long lasting immunity. This is why all French children are offered MMR at 12–15 months and again at 3–6 years.

As such, the main argument for the French system is that it seeks to protect very young infants who may be at greater risk of contracting measles by dint of the greater exposure to others.

The main argument against is that it would increase the number of injections here. There is also some evidence that the immune response to MMR is higher at 12–15 months, if not preceded by a single dose of measles vaccine.

See also paragraphs 5.13 *et seq* and 5.22 *et seq*.

7.1   Was the MMR vaccine adequately tested?

7.2   Will the standard of "the time" and the follow-up meet the concerns in respect of a longer and somewhat newer condition such as regressive autism and autistic spectrum disorder?

The HCCC report acknowledges that the "CSM and MCA reviewed the licensing procedures following the critical paper by Wakefield and Montgomery, and concluded that licensing followed normal procedures, clinical trials met satisfactory standards of the time and follow-up of patients was in accordance with usual practice in vaccine trials".

The evidence reviewed by the Expert Group also supports the conclusion that MMR was appropriately and rigorously tested before introduction, consistent with standards and science relevant at the time. The Expert Group notes that the process has subsequently been formally reviewed by the MCA, who confirmed that licensing followed normal procedures, clinical trials met the satisfactory standards of the time and follow-up of patients was in accordance with usual practices on vaccine trials. The Expert Group recognises that the MCA continually monitors the safety of MMR vaccine in clinical practice and, if necessary, updates the Marketing Authorisation and product information if and when relevant new data become available.

The Expert Group recognises that the identification and analysis of conditions which appear to emerge some considerable time after the administration of any medicine, and which may or may not be connected, may require supporting epidemiological evidence.

The Expert Group recommends that Medicines Control Agency should continue to work closely with the European Union, and appropriate corresponding bodies in individual Member States, to improve collaboration and monitoring of vaccine safety.

See also paragraph 4.19 *et seq.*

8.1   Can the absence of an alleged causal link between MMR and autism be conclusive given that changes may be subtle and gradual and that there may be considerable delay in recognising symptoms, with further delay in diagnostic clinics?

The Medical Research Council Review of Autism confirms that:

"A number of expert review groups have considered the specific question of the potential link between MMR vaccination and ASD (the Medical Research Council, the American Medical Association, the Institute of Medicine, USA, the World Health Organization, the American Academy of Pediatrics, the Population and Public Health Branch of Health Canada, and the Irish Department of Health and Children). All of these groups have analysed the published work.

These reviews were unanimous in concluding that a causal link between the MMR vaccine and 'autistic colitis' and ASD was not proven and that current epidemiological evidence did not support this proposed link."

The Expert Group recognises that the phrase *"does not exclude the possibility"* correctly identifies the impossibility of proving a negative. The Expert Group recognises that, at any given time, governments, organisations and individuals base decisions on the body of scientific evidence that is available at the time. It acknowledges, like the HCCC, the MRC and others, that on the basis of currently available evidence, there is no proven scientific link between the MMR vaccine and autism.

See also paragraph 2.15 *et seq*.

8.2   Is the current "spontaneous" reporting system for vaccines consistent, accurate and "complete" in recognising symptoms of autistic behaviour?

The "Yellow Card" system provides an important early warning of suspected adverse reactions to medicines by collating information required to assess the association between the suspected adverse reaction and the medicine. This scheme may identify previously unknown side-effects or indicate that certain known side-effects occur more commonly than previously believed. It may also identify at-risk groups of patients for particular adverse reactions. Such findings can lead to changes in the marketing authorisation, for example restrictions in use, refinement of dose instructions or the introduction of specific warnings of side-effects in product information, which allow medicines to be used more safely and effectively.

The "Yellow Card" scheme does not act as a register for all adverse reactions (side-effects) that occur. As such, it cannot be regarded as a complete record of symptoms of ASD. The Expert Group recognises that the identification and analysis of conditions which appear to emerge some considerable time after the administration of any medicine, and which may or may not be connected, may require supporting epidemiological evidence.

See also paragraphs 4.10 *et seq*.

8.3 Is it likely that all parents would accurately identify these symptoms of autism?

ASD is diagnosed on the basis of qualitative abnormalities in social, communicative and imaginative behaviours, and the presence of repetitive and stereotyped patterns of interests and activities. Diagnosis is complicated by the varied manifestation of these core deficits, by wide variation in ability level, and by developmental changes.

Parental concern is likely to be a useful indicator of early behavioural difficulties, and it is important that health professionals recognise that parental concern is, in effect, one of the available diagnostic tools.

See also paragraph 2.43 *et seq*.

Next Steps

6.3   The Expert Group's task was to:

a) describe the consequences of pursuing an alternative vaccination policy to MMR;

b) review evidence on the apparent rise in the incidence of autism, taking account of the current work of the Medical Research Council;

c) describe the process of vaccine testing and the monitoring of adverse effects; and

d) in all its work, have regard to the role and remit of the Joint Committee on Vaccination and Immunisation, the Committee on Safety of Medicines and the Medicines Control Agency.

6.4   In the course of addressing that remit, the Expert Group identified a range of possible and desirable changes to existing arrangements. The Group therefore recommends that:

a) The Scottish Executive and the Medical Research Council should work together to drive forward and fund, as appropriate, the full research agenda outlined in the final chapter of the MRC Review of Autism Research, which was informed by the concerns of parents and consumers. Parents and other representatives of those with autism must continue to play a key role in developing research strategies (paragraph 2.40);

b) The Scottish Executive and the Medical Research Council should, in pursuing that research agenda, seek to maximise international collaboration (paragraph 2.41);

c) The Scottish Executive should consult widely, in order to publish a firm timetable for addressing all of the detailed recommendations set out in the *PHIS Autistic Spectrum Disorders Needs Assessment Report* (paragraphs 2.48 and 2.49), and in particular those relating to the:

- development and implementation of improved evidence-based approaches to the diagnosis and management of ASD;

- integrated joint planning, delivery and review of related health, education and social care services, for children, parents and adults, in which context people with autism, or parents and other representatives of those with autism, should have a role;

- need for a more coherent and systematic approach to training health, education and social care professionals, better and in appropriate numbers;

- development of a database of people with ASD in Scotland.

d) The Scottish Executive and the Medical Research Council should work together to drive forward and fund, as appropriate, further research into inflammatory bowel disorders in children (paragraph 3.16).

e) The Medicines Control Agency should continue to work closely with the European Union, and appropriate corresponding bodies in individual Member States, to improve collaboration and monitoring of vaccine safety issues, and regularly review the operation, management and voluntary nature of the "Yellow Card" system in the light of such developments (paragraph 4.18).

f) The Scottish Executive should ensure that (paragraph 4.35):

- vaccination records relating to individual patients should include details of the name and batch number of the vaccine administered;

- a national lifelong vaccination record is developed, to allow identification of the immunisation status of an individual throughout the health service – irrespective of age group and independent of setting;

- NHS Health Boards put in place adequate quality assurance mechanisms to ensure accuracy and completeness of recording of vaccination data.

g) The Committee on Safety of Medicines and the Joint Committee on Vaccination and Immunisation should, taking account of ongoing and future research into the causes of IBD and autism, continue to keep vaccination contraindications under review (paragraph 5.25).

h) The Joint Committee on Vaccination and Immunisation should (paragraph 5.29):

- develop and publish core principles for immunisation policy in order to provide all interested parties with a clear framework against which future policy options might be assessed in an open and transparent manner; and

- continue to publish the conclusion of its regular reviews of the scientific evidence relating to the safety and efficacy of MMR, and seek to improve upon existing arrangements for publicising that material.

i) Health Ministers (in the UK Government and devolved administrations) should urgently implement existing plans to extend arrangements for appointing members to the Joint Committee on Vaccination and Immunisation who are non-medical experts and/or members of the general public (paragraph 5.31).

j) The Scottish Executive should take steps to improve the level and quality of information available to parents whose children are due to be immunised against measles, mumps and rubella (paragraphs 5.21 and 5.32), by:

- ensuring that all parents receive basic factual information about MMR (for example, contraindications, the risks posed by measles, mumps and rubella, and the risks of adverse reactions) with the invitation to bring their child for vaccination;

- ensuring that all parents know that they can and should discuss any related questions with their GP or health visitor in order to make an informed choice about vaccination;

- asking HEBS to evaluate and develop *"the MMR discussion pack"*, in order to maintain and enhance the currency and accuracy of the information, training and support provided to GPs and other health professionals, in relation to the medical science underpinning the immunisation programme;

- requiring NHS Boards to put in place systematic arrangements for providing further advice to parents who, despite discussions with their GP or other health professional, have concerns and questions about MMR or the particular circumstances of their child.

k) The Scottish Executive should ensure that appropriate resources are provided to allow the Scottish Centre for Infection and Environmental Health to carry forward research, in collaboration with the University of Strathclyde, with the aim of developing mathematical models, which might help demonstrate the range of possible outcomes, for the population as a whole, arising out of immunisation decisions made by individual parents (paragraph 5.47).

Annex 1– Membership of the Expert Group

The Very Revd Graham Forbes, Chairman, Provost, St Mary's Cathedral, Edinburgh.

Dr Kenneth Aitken, Child Clinical Neuro-Psychologist.

Dr Gordon Bell, Lovass Technique Advisor.

Dr J Claire Bramley, Epidemiologist, Scottish Centre for Infection and Environmental Health.

Dr Clare Brogan, Lecturer, Department of Psychology, Glasgow Caledonian University; Representative of the National Autistic Society.

Dr David Cromie, Consultant in Public Health Medicine, Lanarkshire Health Board.

Mr Martyn Evans, Director, Scottish Consumer Council.

Dr David Goldblatt, Reader in Immunology, Immunobiology Unit, Institute of Child Health, University of London.

Mrs Gillian Hamer-Hodges, National Association for Colitis and Crohn's Disease.

Mrs Jane Hook, Chair, Scottish Society on Autism.

Professor Steve Hudson, Professor of Pharmaceutical Care, Strathclyde University.

Professor Eve Johnston CBE, Professor of Psychiatry, University of Edinburgh; Chair of Medical Research Council Autism Review.

Ms Jo McCallum, Public Health Nurse Specialist, Department of Public Health, Ayrshire and Arran Health Board.

Dr Adrian Margerison, Chairman, Scottish Association of Community Child Health.

Dr Andrew Riley, Director of Public Health, Borders NHS Board.

Professor Lewis Ritchie, General Practitioner; Head of Department of General Practice and Primary Care, University of Aberdeen; Professor of General Practice, University of Aberdeen.

Mr Bruce Robertson, Director of Education, Culture and Sport, Highland Council.

Professor Lawrence Weaver, Samson Gemmell Professor and Head of the Department of Child Health, University of Glasgow.

Mr Jonathon Best, Chief Executive of Yorkhill NHS Trust, was originally a member of the Group. He withdrew in January 2002, when it became clear that other commitments would continue to prevent him from participating fully in the process.

Summary of Declared Interests

	Interests of a financial, lobby/political, scientific (research funding), litigation, family or other personal nature	Interests relating to, for example, employment	Other
Dr K Aitken	• Employed as an independent Consultant Child Clinical Neuro-psychologist, and part time by Greater Glasgow Primary Healthcare Trust. • Research interests include the Intercontinental Case Control Study of Autism, and work with the Repligen Corporation, Laxdale Pharmaceuticals and the Sackler Foundation. • Expert witness in current legal action relating to MMR vaccine and autism, remunerated by Legal Aid Board. • No other relevant registerable financial interests, including shares.	None.	Member of the Biomedical sub-group of the Scottish Parliament Cross-party Group on Autistic Spectrum Disorders.
Dr G Bell	• Son has ASD. • Employed solely by the University of Stirling; activity includes research funded by the Autism Research Trust; no other relevant registerable financial interests, including shares. • Lead applicant on a research proposal to SEHD-CSO.	The University of Stirling has a diverse set of roles and functions relating to teaching, research, and the appropriate commercialisation of that work. The University therefore has related contractual, administrative and financial arrangements with Government, Research Councils, charitable organisations and businesses.	Chairman of the Biomedical sub-group of the Scottish Parliament Cross-party Group on Autistic Spectrum Disorders.

	Interests of a financial, lobby/political, scientific (research funding), litigation, family or other personal nature	Interests relating to, for example, employment	Other
Dr J C Bramley	• Employed solely by SCIEH; no other relevant registerable financial interests, including shares. • Member of PHLS Advisory Committee on Vaccines and Immunisation.	• The Scottish Centre for Infection and Environmental Health (SCIEH) is a division of the Common Services Agency (CSA) for NHSScotland. SCIEH has a diverse set of roles and responsibilities relating to the national surveillance of communicable diseases and environmental hazards, and the provision of expert support to practitioners, policy-makers and others on infection and environmental health. These include immunisation and vaccine-preventable diseases. • The CSA and SCIEH receive contracts, research funding and other income from Government, charitable organisations and pharmaceutical companies, including those with an interest in vaccines.	None.

	Interests of a financial, lobby/political, scientific (research funding), litigation, family or other personal nature	Interests relating to, for example, employment	Other
Dr C Brogan	• Employed by Glasgow Caledonian University and by the University of Strathclyde (on a part-time basis). Previously employed by the National Autistic Society (NAS); no other relevant registerable financial interests, including shares. • Member of the PHIS working group which prepared the SNAP report on autistic spectrum disorders. • Lead applicant on a research proposal to SEHD-CSO (pilot study to develop a register of children with ASD).	• Glasgow Caledonian University has a diverse set of roles and functions relating to teaching, research and the appropriate commercialisation of that work. The University therefore has related contractual, administrative and financial arrangements with Government, Research Councils, charitable organisations and businesses. • The National Autistic Society is a registered charity which champions the rights and interests of all people with autism and their families and ensures that they receive quality services appropriate to their needs.	None.
Dr D Cromie	Employed solely as a Consultant in Public Health Medicine by Lanarkshire NHS Board; no other relevant registerable financial interests, including shares.	Lanarkshire NHS Board has a diverse set of roles and responsibilities relating to the delivery of health services within its boundaries. These include immunisation, and the diagnosis and treatment of autistic spectrum disorders.	None.
Mr M Evans	Employed solely as Director of the Scottish Consumer Council; Visiting Professor of Law at University of Strathclyde (unpaid) to 31 December 2001; no other relevant registerable financial interests, including shares.	The Scottish Consumer Council is part of a non-profit making company. It is independent of any commercial, political or other vested interest.	Member of several SEHD advisory groups.

	Interests of a financial, lobby/political, scientific (research funding), litigation, family or other personal nature	Interests relating to, for example, employment	Other
Very Revd G Forbes	Provost, St Mary's Cathedral, Edinburgh; Member, General Medical Council; Member, the Clinical Standards Board for Scotland; no other relevant registerable financial interests, including shares.	St Mary's Cathedral, Edinburgh has shares in GlaxoSmithKline.	None.
Dr D Goldblatt	• Reader/honorary consultant at the Institute of Child Health and Great Ormond Street Hospital, London. • Additional income derived from consultancy and other work for a range of companies, including GlaxoSmithKline and Wyeth Lederle Vaccines; also providing expert reports for solicitors representing a company that manufactures MMR. • No shares which qualify as relevant registerable financial interests.	The Institute of Child Health has interests in teaching, research and supporting service developments. It therefore has related contractual, administrative and financial arrangements with Government, Research Councils, charitable organisations and businesses.	Member of JCVI.

	Interests of a financial, lobby/political, scientific (research funding), litigation, family or other personal nature	Interests relating to, for example, employment	Other
Mrs G Hamer-Hodges	<ul><li>Son has Crohn's disease.</li><li>Member of National Association for Colitis and Crohn's Disease (NACC).</li><li>No relevant registerable financial interests, including shares or employment.</li></ul>	<ul><li>The NACC is a registered charity which provides medical information, practical help and emotional support for people who have been diagnosed with IBD and for their families. It offers a welfare grant to those suffering financial difficulty as a direct result of IBD.</li><li>NACC receives some sponsorship from GlaxoSmithKline, Astra Zeneca and others.</li></ul>	None.
Mrs J Hook	<ul><li>Daughter has ASD.</li><li>Chair of Scottish Society for Autism.</li><li>Member of the PHIS working group which prepared the SNAP report on autistic spectrum disorders.</li><li>No relevant registerable financial interests, including shares.</li></ul>	The Scottish Society for Autism is a registered charity which seeks to ensure the provision of the best education, care, support and opportunities for people of all ages with autism in Scotland.	Member of steering group on review of psychological services. Vice-convenor Cross-party Group on ASD.

	Interests of a financial, lobby/political, scientific (research funding), litigation, family or other personal nature	Interests relating to, for example, employment	Other
Professor S Hudson	• Employed solely by Strathclyde University as Boots Professor of Pharmaceutical Care. The chair has been endowed since 1997 by the Boots company for five years. The terms of the endowment mean that the charitable contribution to the University carries no obligations to the donors. • No other relevant registerable financial interests, including shares.	Strathclyde University has a diverse set of roles and functions relating to teaching, research, and the appropriate commercialisation of that work. The University therefore has related contractual, administrative and financial arrangements with Government, Research Councils, charitable organisations and businesses.	None.
Professor E Johnston CBE	• Employed by Edinburgh University as Professor of Psychiatry; research programme funded by the Medical Research Council; paid honorarium by Medical Research Council as Chairman of the MRC Neurosciences Board. • Chair of the MRC Autism Review. • Member of a number of professional organisations. • Shares in GlaxoSmithKline; no other relevant registerable financial interests.	• Edinburgh University has a diverse set of roles and functions relating to teaching, research and the appropriate commercialisation of that work. The University therefore has related contractual, administrative and financial arrangements with Government, Research Councils, charitable organisations and businesses. • The Dept of Psychiatry has interests in teaching, research and supporting service developments.	None.

	Interests of a financial, lobby/political, scientific (research funding), litigation, family or other personal nature	Interests relating to, for example, employment	Other
Ms J McCallum	Employed solely as a Public Health Nurse Specialist by Arran and Ayrshire NHS Board; no relevant registerable financial interests, including shares.	Arran and Ayrshire NHS Board has a diverse set of roles and responsibilities relating to the delivery of health services within its boundaries. These include immunisation, and the diagnosis and treatment of autistic spectrum disorders.	None.
Dr A Margerison	Employed solely by Borders NHS Board; Chairman of Scottish Association of Community Child Health; no relevant registerable financial interests, including shares.	Borders NHS Board has a diverse set of roles and responsibilities relating to the delivery of health services within its boundaries. These include immunisation, and the diagnosis and treatment of autistic spectrum disorders. The Board has interests in teaching, research and supporting service developments.	None.
Dr A Riley	• Employed solely as Director of Public Health by Borders NHS Board. • Member of Faculty of Public Health Medicine and Borders Research Ethics Committee. • Shares in GlaxoSmithKline; no other relevant registerable financial interests.		None.

	Interests of a financial, lobby/political, scientific (research funding), litigation, family or other personal nature	Interests relating to, for example, employment	Other
Professor L Ritchie	• James Mackenzie Professor and Head of the Department of General Practice and Primary Care at the University of Aberdeen; General Practitioner Principal at Peterhead Health Centre; Honorary Consultant in Public Health Medicine, Grampian Health Board. • Lectures/seminars sponsored by pharmaceutical companies, on an irregular basis. • No relevant registerable financial interests, including shares.	University Department has interests in teaching, research and supporting service developments in general practice and primary care. This includes medicines assessment/drug trial work sponsored by pharmaceutical companies.	• JCVI member. • Membership of several SEHD advisory groups.
Mr B Robertson	• Employed solely as Director of Education Culture and Sport, Highland Council; no relevant registerable financial interests, including shares. • Member of several SE advisory groups.	Highland Council has a diverse set of roles and responsibilities relating to the delivery of services within its boundaries. These include supporting immunisation of school-age children, and the provision of appropriate education and social services for those with autistic spectrum disorders.	None.
Professor L Weaver	• Employed by Glasgow University as Head of Dept of Child Health and by Royal Hospital for Sick Children. • Member of a number of professional organisations and research/advisory committees. • Shares in GlaxoSmithKline; no other relevant registerable financial interests.	The University of Glasgow has a diverse set of roles and functions relating to teaching, research and the appropriate commercialisation of that work. The University therefore has related contractual, administrative and financial arrangements with Government, Research Councils, charitable organisations and businesses.	None.

Annex 2 – Policy in European Countries – EU and Norway and Switzerland – taken from Euvax Project Report

The Scientific and Technical Evaluation of Vaccination Programmes in the European Union – known as the EUVAX Project Report – summarises the findings from immunisation programmes in 17 European countries – the 15 EU Member States plus Norway and Switzerland.

Country	Included in Vaccination Programme			
	MMR vaccine	Measles vaccine	Mumps vaccine	Rubella vaccine
Austria	YES	NO	NO	YES For special groups
Belgium	YES	NO	NO	NO
Denmark	YES	NO	NO	YES
Finland	YES	NO	NO	NO
France	YES	YES For special groups	NO	YES For special groups
Germany	YES	NO	NO	NO
Greece	YES	YES For special groups	YES For special groups	YES For special groups
Ireland	YES	NO	NO	NO
Italy	YES	YES	YES For special groups	YES For special groups
Luxembourg	YES	NO	NO	YES For special groups
Netherlands	YES	NO	NO	NO
Norway	YES	NO	NO	NO
Portugal	YES	INFORMATION NOT HELD	NO	NO
Spain	YES	NO	NO	NO
Sweden	YES	NO	NO	NO
Switzerland	YES	NO	NO	NO
UK	YES	NO	NO	YES For special groups

Uptake in European Countries

Information on programme monitoring from the EUVAX report indicates in which countries coverage is assessed but does not provide information on uptake rates.

Annex 3 – Costs

All members of the group gave their time voluntarily. However, there were costs involved in both preparing and producing this report, as shown below. Actual costs are as at 31 March 2002, with subsequent expenditure (such as printing) included as estimates.

Type	Explanation	Amount (£000s)
Accommodation/ travel expenses	Costs of accommodation and travel	10.9
Presenters' travel expenses	As above for those individuals/organisations who presented evidence to the Group	1.1
Advertising costs	Advertisements were placed in the Health Service Journal, Aberdeen Press & Journal, Scotsman, Herald and Daily Record, inviting written contributions from individuals and organisations appropriately cross referenced to the Group's remit	6.5
Parents' and Health Professional Groups	As part of the process of consultation, the Expert Group established a Parents' Reference Group to inform deliberations of the Expert Group by identifying priority issues relevant to its remit and providing constructive comment on the draft report. Scottish Health Feedback, an independent research organisation, was contracted to manage this task	15.8
Printing costs	Estimate	14.1
TOTAL		**48.4**

Annex 4 – Glossary of Terms

Generally, the Expert Group has tried to define terms in the body of the Report. However, for ease of reference, some of the terms and abbreviations used are set out below:

Antigen – the term applied to a substance which causes the formation of antibodies: that is, bodies which act in opposition to poisons formed in the body or introduced from outside.

Asperger syndrome – characterised by the same type of abnormalities in reciprocal social interaction and restricted, stereotyped, repetitive patterns of interests and activities that typify autistic disorder; *however*, it differs primarily in that there is no clinically significant delay in spoken or receptive language or in cognitive development. There is no requirement to have had developmental difficulties before 3 years of age (AS).

Atypical autism – the term used when a disorder differs from classical autism due to a later age of onset (at or after 3 years), atypical or sub-threshold symptoms (typical age of onset, but without a full clinical presentation), or all of these (atypical for both age of onset and clinical presentation). This category is sometimes referred to as "pervasive developmental disorders – not otherwise specified" (PDD–NOS).

Childhood (classical) autism – defined by the presence of abnormal or impaired development that is manifest before the age of 3 years, and the characteristic type of abnormal functioning in all three areas of the triad of impairments. DSM-IV defines this as autistic disorder (AD).

CSM – Committee on Safety of Medicines – one of the independent advisory committees established under the Medicines Act. It advises Health Ministers on the quality, efficacy and safety of medicines in order to ensure that appropriate public health standards are met and maintained.

DSM – Diagnostic and Statistical Manual – an internationally accepted framework for diagnosis of developmental disorders, including ASD.

Efficacy – measure of the degree to which the desired effect is achieved.

Encephalitis – inflammation of the brain. It is usually caused by a virus infection, and may occur as a complication of the common infectious diseases, including measles.

Environmental risk factors – all factors which are not genetic.

Epidemiology – the study of the incidence and distribution of diseases, and other factors relating to health.

HCCC – the Health and Community Care Committee of the Scottish Parliament.

Heritable – transmissible from parent to offspring.

ICD-10 – International Classification of Diseases – guidance from the World Health Organization – an internationally accepted framework for diagnosis of developmental disorders, including ASD.

IBD – Inflammatory Bowel Disease – the collective name for Crohn's disease and ulcerative colitis, which are chronic conditions in which the intestines and the large bowel, respectively, become swollen, inflamed and ulcerated.

Incidence – a measure of the development of "new" cases of a condition.

JCVI – the Joint Committee on Vaccination and Immunisation – the statutory expert Standing Advisory Committee which advises Health Ministers on matters relating to communicable diseases, preventable, and potentially preventable, through immunisation.

MCA – UK Medicines Control Agency – an Executive Agency of the Department of Health. Its primary objective is to safeguard public health by ensuring that all medicines on the UK market meet appropriate standards of safety, quality and efficacy.

MMR – combined measles, mumps and rubella vaccine.

MRC – UK Medical Research Council.

Otitis media – an infection of the middle ear.

Risk – the possibility of more than one outcome occurring. A more relevant definition, in the context of public health issues, acknowledges the Executive's duty to identify hazards which, by dint of their nature or scale, require some form of intervention in the best interests of the public. The focus is therefore on the possibility of harmful or negative outcomes.

> Risk = hazard X exposure,

where a hazard is something with the potential to cause an adverse effect.

Pathogenic – disease producing, or capable of causing disease.

Peer-review – the method by which research is quality assured, given the often highly specialised nature of cutting-edge research. Essentially, before a research paper is published, it is examined by other scientists working within that discipline or subject area, to ensure that the design, methodology, process, interpretation and description of results are sound.

Pharmacovigilance – the process of monitoring medicines as used in everyday practice to identify previously unrecognised or changes in the patterns of their adverse effects, and assessing the risks and taking account of the benefits of medicines in order to determine what action, if any, is necessary to improve their safe use.

PHIS – Public Health Institute of Scotland.

Prevalence – A measure of the number of individuals with a condition at a point in time or over a defined period.

SCIEH – Scottish Centre for Infection and Environmental Health.

Annex 5 – References

[1]Taylor B *et al*. Autism and measles, mumps and rubella vaccine: no epidemiological evidence for a causal association. *Lancet* 353, 2026–2029 (1999).

Farrington CP Miller E & Taylor B. MMR and autism: further evidence against a causal association. *Vaccine* 19, 3632–3635 (2001).

Smeeth L *et al*. A case-control study of autism and mumps-measles-rubella vaccination using the general practice research database: design and methodology. *BMC. Public Health* 1, 2 (2001).

Smeeth L *et al*. Measles, mumps, and rubella (MMR) vaccine and autism. Ecological studies cannot answer main question. *BMJ* 323, 163 (2001).

DeWilde S, Carey I M, Richards N, Hilton SR & Cook DG. Do children who become autistic consult more often after MMR vaccination? *Br. J. Gen. Pract.* 51, 226-227 (2001). mucosa to gluten challenge in autistic subjects. *Lancet* 2, 877–878 (1979).

Fombonne E & Chakrabarti S. No evidence for a new variant of MMR-induced autism. *Pediatrics* (2001).

Dales L, Hammer SJ & Smith NJ. Time trends in autism and in MMR immunization coverage in California. *JAMA* 285,1183–1185 (2001).

Kaye JA, Mar Melero-Montes M & Jick H. Mumps, measles, and rubella vaccine and the incidence of autism recorded by general practitioners: a time trend analysis. *BMJ* 322, 460–463 (2001).

[2]Medical Research Council. Report of the Strategy Development Group Subgroup on Research into Bowel Disorders and Autism. London, England, Medical Research Council. www.mrc.ac.uk/Autism_report.html (2000).

American Medical Association. Current scientific data do not support causal association between autism and the MMR vaccine. American Medical Association. www.ama-assn.org/ama/pub/article/1824-2080.html (2000).

Stratton K. Immunization safety review: measles-mumps rubella vaccine and autism. Institute of Medicine. 2001. Washington DC, National Academy Press. www.iom.edu/IOM/IOMHome.nsf/Pages/MMR+and+Autism (2001).

World Health Organization. Adverse Events following measles-mumps and rubella vaccines. www.who.int/vaccines-diseases/safety/infobank/mmr.html (2000).

Halsey NA & Hyman SL. Measles-mumps-rubella vaccine and autistic spectrum disorder: Report from the New Challenges in Childhood Immunizations Conference convened in Oak Brook, Illinois, June 12–13, 2000. *Pediatrics* 107, E84 (2001).

Strauss B & Bigham M. Does measles-mumps-rubella (MMR) vaccination cause inflammatory bowel disease and autism? *Can. Commun. Dis. Rep.* 27, 65–72 (2001).

Irish Department of Health and Children. Irish Department of Health and Children. www.gov.ie/committees-01/c-health/rep-childhood/default.htm (2001).

[3]Report on inquiry into issues surrounding the alleged relationship between the combined measles, mumps and rubella vaccine and autism. 2001.

[4]Scottish Executive response to the Report on inquiry into issues surrounding the alleged relationship between the combined measles, mumps and rubella vaccine and autism. http://www.scotland.gov.uk

[5]Guidelines 2000: Scientific Advice And Policy Making. The Office of Science and Technology. July 2000. www.dti.gov.uk/ost/aboutost/guidelines.htm

[6]The MMR Discussion Pack. Health Education Board for Scotland. September 2001. ISBN 1-902030-26-5. http://www.hebs.scot.nhs.uk

[7]Rothman KJ and Greenland S. Causation and causal interference from Modern Epidemiology. 2nd Edn. 1998.

[8]MRC Review of Autism Research. December 2001. www.mrc.ac.uk

[9]Autistic Spectrum Disorders Needs Assessment Report. Public Health Institute for Scotland. December 2001. ISBN 1-904196-02. www.show.scot.nhs.uk/PHIS

[10]World Health Organization. ICD-10 Classification of mental and behavioural disorders: clinical description and diagnostic guidelines. WHO 1994.

[11]American Psychiatric Association. *Diagnostic and Statistical Manual of Mental Disorders.* 4th Edn (DSM-IV). APA 1994.

[12]Wing L, Gould J. Severe impairments of social interaction and associated abnormalities in Children: epidemiology and classification. *Journal of Autism and Developmental Disorders.* 9 (1), 11–29 (1979).

[13]Wing L. The definition and prevalence of autism: a review. *European Child and Adolescent Psychiatry* 2 (2), 61-74 (1993).

[14]Ehlers S, Gillberg C. The epidemiology of Asperger Syndrome. A total population study. *Journal of Child Psychology and Psychiatry.* 34 (8); 1327–1350 (1993).

[15]Fombonne E. The epidemiology of autism: a review. *Psychological Medicine.* 29 (4), 769–786 (1999).

[16]Gillberg C, Wing L. Autism: not an extremely rare disorder. *Acta Psychiatrica Scandinavica*. June 1999 (6), 399–406 (1999).

[17]Powell JE, Edwards A, Edwards M, Pandit BS, Sungum-Paliwal SR, Whitehouse W. Changes in the incidence of childhood autism and other autistic spectrum disorders in preschool children from two areas of the West Midlands, UK. *Developmental Medicine and Child Neurology*. 42 (9), 624–628 (2000).

[18]Baird *et al*. A screening instrument for Autism at 18 months of age: a six-year follow-up study. *Journal American Academy of Child & Adolescent Psychiatry*. 39 (6), 694–702 (2000).

[19]Center for Disease Control and Prevention. Prevalence of Autism in Brick Township, New Jersey 1998: Community Report. Atlanta, GA: Center for Disease Control and Prevention. 2000.

[20]Chakrabarti S, Fombonne E. Pervasive developmental disorders in preschool children. *Journal of the American Medical Association*. (2000).

[21]Morris A, Aldulaimi D. New evidence for a viral pathogenic mechanism for new variant inflammatory bowel disease and development disorder? *J. Clin. Pathol.: Mol. Pathol.* 55, 0 (2002).

[22]Table taken from MRC presentation to the MMR Expert Group, January 2002. See http://www.show.scot.nhs.uk/mmrexpertgroup/.

[23]Bailey A *et al*. Autism as a strongly genetic disorder: evidence from a British twin study. *Psychol. Med*. 25, 63–77 (1995).

[24]Rutter M, Silberg J, O'Connor T, & Simonoff E. genetic and child psychiatry: II Empirical research findings. *J. Child Psychol. Psychiatry*. 40, 19– 55 (1999).

[25]May M. Disturbing behaviour: neurotoxic effects in children. *Environ. Health Perspect*. 108, A262–A267 (2000).

[26]Wakefield AJ. *et al*. Ileal-lymphoid-nodular hyperplasia, nonspecific colitis, and pervasive developmental disorder in children. *Lancet* 351, 637–641 (1998).

[27]Taylor B, Miller E, Lingam R, Andrews N, Simmons A, Stowe J. Measles, mumps, and rubella vaccination and bowel problems or developmental regression in children with autism: population study. *BMJ*. 324, 393-396 (2002).

[28]Peltola H. *et al*. No evidence for measles, mumps, and rubella vaccine-associated inflammatory bowel disease or autism in a 14-year prospective study. *Lancet* 351, 1327–1328 (1998).

[29]Uhlmann V, Martin CM, Sheils O, Pilkington L, Silva I, Killalea A, Murch SB, Wakefield AJ , O'Leary JJ. Potential viral pathogenic mechanism for new variant inflammatory bowel disease. *Clin J, Pathol, Mol Pathol,* 55, 0–6 (2002).

[30]Akobeng AK, & Thomas AG. Inflammatory bowel disease, autism and the measles, mumps and rubella vaccine. *Journal of Pediatric Gastroenterology and Nutrition* 28, 351–352 (1999).

Fombonne E, Chakrabarti S. No evidence for a new variant of measles-mumps-rubella-induced autism. *Pediatrics* 108, E58 (2001).

Horvath K, Papadimitriou JC, Rabsztyn A, Drachenberg C, Tildon JT. Gastrointestinal abnormalities in children with autistic disorder. *J. Pediatr* 135, 559–63 (1999).

Taylor B, Miller E, Lingam R, Andrews N, Simmons A, Stowe J. Measles, mumps, and rubella vaccination and bowel problems or developmental regression in children with autism: population study. *BMJ* 324, 393–396 (2002).

Wakefield AJ, Anthony A, Murch SH, Thomson M, Montgomery SM, Davies S, O'Leary JJ, Berelowitz M, Walker-Smith JA. Enterocolitis in children with developmental disorders. *Am. J. Gastroenterol.* 95, 2285–2295 (2000).

[31]Wing L. The Autistic Spectrum – A guide for parents and professionals. London: Constable and Co Ltd. 1996.

Jordan R. The nature and definition of Autism. Autistic Spectrum Disorders: An introductory handbook for practitioners. David Fulton Publishers Ltd: London 1999.

[32]Community Care: A Joint Future. The Report of the Joint Futures Group. http://www.scotland.gov.uk/health/ltc/Documents/jointresourcing.pdf

[33]Lapidus A. The changing epidemology of IBD. *Acta. Gastroenterol. Belg.* 2001; 64; 155-9.

[34]Sawczenko *et al.* Prospective survey of childhood IBD in the British isles. *Lancet* 2001; 357; 1093.

[35]Barton *et al.* Incidence of IBD in Scottish Children between 1968-83; Marginal fall in ulcerative colitis; three-fold increase in Crohn's disease. *Gut* 1989; 30; 618-22.

Armitage *et al.* Incidence of juvenile-onset Crohn's disease in Scotland. *Lancet* 1999; 353; 1496-7.

[36]Armitage *et al.* Increasing evidence of both juvenile-onset Crohn's disease and ulcerative colitis in Scotland. *Eur. J. Gastroenterol Hepatol.* 2001; 13; 1439-47.

[37]Ahmad T, Satsangi J, McGovern D, Bunce M, Jewell DP. The genetics of inflammatory bowel disease. *Aliment. Pharmacol. Therap.* 15, 731–738 (2001).

[38]Ogura Y, Bonen DK, Inohara N., Nicolae DL, Chen FF, Ramos R *et al*. A frameshift mutation in NOD2 associated with susceptibility to Crohn's disease. *Nature*. 411, 603–606 (2001).

[39]Hugot J-P, Chamaillard M, Zonali H, Lesage S, Cezard J-P, Belaiche J *et al*. Association of NOD-2 leucine rich repeat variants with susceptibility to Crohn's disease. *Nature* 411, 599–603 (2001).

[40]Hampe J, Cuthbert A, Croucher P J et al. Association between insertion mutation in NOD2 gene and Crohn's disease in German and British populations. *Lancet* 357, 1925–1928 (2001).

[41]Wakefield AJ, Pittilo RM, Sim R, *et al*. Evidence of persistent measles virus infection in Crohn's disease. *J. Med. Virol*. 39, 345–353 (1993).

[42]Iizuka M, Chiba M, Yukawa M, Nakagomi T, Fukushima T, Watanabe S, Nakagomi O. Immunohistochemical analysis of the distribution of measles related antigen in the intestinal mucosa in inflammatory bowel disease. *Gut* 46, 163–169 (2000).

Afzal MA, Minor PD, Schild GC. Clinical safety issues of measles, mumps and rubella vaccines. *Bulletin of the World Health Organization* 78,199–204 (2000).

[43]Chadwick N, Bruce IJ, Schepelmann S, Pounder RE, Wakefield AJ. Measles virus RNA is not detected in inflammatory bowel disease using hybrid capture and reverse transcription followed by the polymerase chain reaction. J. Med. Virol. 55, 305–311 (1998).

[44]Ekbom A, Wakefield AJ, Zack M, Adami HO. Perinatal measles infection and subsequent Crohn's disease. *Lancet* 344: 508–510 (1994).

Ekbom A, Daszak P, Kraaz W, Wakefield AJ. Crohn's disease after in-utero measles virus exposure. *Lancet* 348, 515–517 (1996).

Ekbom A, Wakefield AJ, Zack M, Adami HO. Perinatal measles infection and subsequent Crohn's disease. *Lancet* 344, 508–510 (1994).

Thompson NP, Montgomery SM, Pounder RE, Wakefield AJ. Is measles vaccination a risk factor for inflammatory bowel disease? *Lancet* 345, 1071–1074 (1995).

Thompson NP, Pounder RE, Wakefield AJ. Perinatal and childhood risk factors for inflammatory bowel disease: a case-control study. *European Journal of Gastroenterology and Hepatology* 7, 385–390 (1995).

[45]Nielsen LLW, Nielsen NM, Melbye M, Sodermann M, Jacobsen M, Aaby P. Exposure to measles in utero and Crohn's disease: Danish register study. *BMJ* 316, 196–197 (1998).

Davis RL, Kramarz P, Bohlke K, Benson P, Thompson RS, Mullooly J *et al*. Measles-mumps-rubella and other measles-containing vaccines do not increase the risk for inflammatory bowel disease: a case-control study from the Vaccine Safety Datalink project. *Archives of Pediatric and Adolescent Medicine* 155, 354–359 (2001).

[46]Wakefield AJ *et al*. Ileal-lymphoid-nodular hyperplasia, non-specific colitis and pervasive developmental disorder in children. *Lancet* 351, 637–641 (1998).

[47]Wakefield AJ *et al*. Enterocolitis in children with developmental disorders. *Am. J. Gastroenterol.* 95, 2285–2295 (2000).

[48]Wakefield AJ & Montgomery SM. Measles, mumps and rubella vaccine: through a glass darkly. *Adverse Drug Reactions and Toxicological Reviews* 19(4), 265–283 (2000).

[49]Arlett P, Bryan P. A response to "Measles, mumps and rubella vaccine: through a glass darkly". *Adverse Drug Reactions and Toxicological Reviews* 20(1), 37–45 (2001).

[50]Miller E, Waight P, Farrington CP, Andrews N, Stowe J, Taylor B. Idiopathic thrombocytopenic purpura and MMR vaccine. Arch. Dis. Child. 84, 227–229 (2001).

[51]Miller CL. Severity of notified measles. *BMJ* 1, 1253 (1978).

[52]Miller CL. Deaths from measles in England and Wales, 1970–83. *BMJ* 290, 443–444 (1985).

[53]Miller C, Farrington CP, Harbert K. The epidemiology of subacute sclerosing panencephalitis in England and Wales 1970–1989. *International Journal of Epidemiology* 21(5), 998-1006 (1992).

[54]Centers for Disease Control and Prevention. Epidemiology and Prevention of Vaccine-Preventable Diseases. 6th Edn. 2001.

[55]Centers for Disease Control and Prevention. Measles Outbreak – Netherlands, April 1999–January 2000. *MMWR* 49(14), 299–303 (2000).

[56]McBrien J, Glynn F, O'Donovan C *et al*. An outbreak of measles in Dublin in the year 2000. *Irish Journal of Medical Science* 169(4), 332 (2000).

[57]Galbraith NS, Young SEJ, Pusey JJ, Crombie DL, Sparks JP. Mumps surveillance in England and Wales 1962–81. *Lancet* 1, 91–94 (1984).

[58]Hall R, Richards H. Hearing loss due to mumps. *Archives of Disease in Childhood* 62, 189–191 (1987).

[59]Plotkin SA, Wharton M. Mumps vaccine. In: Plotkin SA, Orenstein WA, eds. Vaccines. Philadelphia: W. B. Saunders, 267–292 (1999).

[60]Miller E, Cradock-Watson JE, Pollock TM. Consequences of confirmed maternal rubella at successive stages of pregnancy. *Lancet* 2, 781–784 (1982).

[61]Panagiotopoulos T, Antoniadou I, Valassi-Adam E. Increase in congenital rubella occurrence after immunisation in Greece: retrospective survey and systematic review (2001). *BMJ* 319, 1462–1467 (1999).

[62]Sir Kenneth Calman in "The Legacy of Jenner", the Foreword to the Immunisation against Infectious Disease 1996. ISBN 0-11-321815-X.

[63]A report on this survey was published in Eurosurveillance Vol. 6, No. 6 June, 2001. See also www.eurosurveillance.org *or* www-nt.who.int/vaccines/globalsummary/Immunization/CountryProfileSelect.cfm

[64]http://www.show.scot.nhs.uk/isd/child_health/ch_immunisation/ch_immunisation.htm

[65]Evans M, Stoddart H, Condon L, Freeman E, Grizzell M, Mullen R. Parents' perspectives on the MMR immunisation: a focus group study. *Br. J. Gen. Pract.* 51, 904–910 (2001).

[66]Offit PA, Quarles J, Gerber MA, Hackett CJ, Marcuse EK, Kollman T, Gellin BG, Landry S. Addressing Parents' Concerns: Do Multiple Vaccines Overwhelm or Weaken the Infant's Immune System. 2002.

[67]1. Measles, Japan, 1999–2001. *IASR* 22, 273–274 (2001). http://idsc.nih.go.jp/iasr/22/261/tpc261.html

2. Akeda H, Kohama M, Ashimine K, et al. An epidemic of measles, September 1998– October 1999 – Okinawa. *IASR* 20, 275 (1999). http://idsc.nih.go.jp/iasr/20/237/de237b.html

3. World Health Organization "Information on programme monitoring from the EUVAX report indicates in which countries coverage is assessed but does not provide information on uptake rates."

[68]Centers for Disease Control and Prevention. Measles Outbreak – Netherlands, April 1999– January 2000. *MMWR* 49(14), 299-303 (2000).

[69]McBrien J, Glynn F, O'Donovan C *et al*. An outbreak of measles in Dublin in the year 2000. *Irish Journal of Medical Science* 169(4), 332 (2000).

[70]Begg N, Nicoll A. Myths in Medicine: Immunisation: Children taking antibiotics shouldn't be vaccinated. *BMJ* 1994; 309: 1073-1075.